THE
CULPITT BOOK
OF
CAKE DECORATION

G.T. Culpitt & Son

First published in Great Britain
by G. T. Culpitt & Son Ltd,
Culpitt House, 74-78 Town Centre,
Hatfield, Herts AL10 0AW

ISBN 0 9510161 0 5

Made by Lennard Books,
Windmill Cottage, Mackerye End,
Harpenden, Herts AL5 5DR
Art Director David Pocknell
Designed by Silk Pearce
Editor Michael Leitch
Photography by Tony Pickhaver
Production Reynolds Clark Associates Ltd
Printed and bound in England by James Cond Printers, Birmingham

CONTENTS

INTRODUCTION

Welcome to *The Culpitt Book of Cake Decoration!*

G.T. Culpitt & Son Ltd was born in 1922. It was started by my grandparents and my parents, who were specialists in the millinery trade and were constantly being requested to produce bouquets for wedding cakes. From a small beginning, the company developed by employing specialists in other fields. One of their main ambitions was that all their products should be of a very high quality and, to this day, that is still our policy.

The company has grown steadily over the years and from modest beginnings with only four people we now employ over 300 in a purpose-built factory which produces over a thousand standard products in the most hygienic conditions.

Over the years, fashions in celebration cakes have changed considerably, and so have the decorations. Although the old traditional themes still flourish, there is also an ever-increasing trend for modern decorations, and we hope you will find in the products illlustrated a tempting selection to suit all occasions.

We have tried in the main to show cakes which are relatively quick and easy to decorate. Some are fairly sophisticated and more suitable for the experienced decorator, while others are intended for the student who needs something uncomplicated. The book is unique in that it also shows a large range of cake decorations that are available through wholesale, retail, and direct mail in the United Kingdom, and through wholesalers in most parts of the western world. It is meant to be a book of ideas, and we are certain that you, our readers, will adopt, adapt and improve on them to match your own needs.

Many outlets stock assorted packs of decoration from which individual lines may be purchased. Reference codes commencing with 'ST' refer to lines only available from these packs; they are not illustrated in the Catalogue section.

David Culpitt

CAKES FOR ALL OCCASIONS

This part of the book is the ideas section. The cakes illustrated have been made by many different decorators in many parts of the world – as far afield as Australia, Canada, Denmark and Singapore.

Together they form a bank of ideas on which you, whether you are an amateur or a professional decorator, can draw for either pleasure or profit, or both.

Naturally, the cakes have been made using various bases, but in the majority of instances your own favourite recipe will be just as suitable. In the same way, the types of icing or coating used on the cakes can be varied to suit your personal preference.

Cake and drum sizes are specified only here and there. This is because most designs can be made in several sizes to suit the occasion. The important thing is to keep the proportions in balance, and for that reason we generally recommend using a cake drum 2in (5cm) larger than the cake.

Another point to note: in some of the designs illustrated you will find that the decorator has taken a standard product apart and used one or more of the components to create a different effect. Many of the decorations shown here and in the Catalogue section offer plenty of scope for this kind of originality. Happy viewing!

A Wedding Day is a very special occasion, and when the time arrives for toasts and speeches the cake becomes a focal point. Custom in the past virtually demanded a white cake, but these days colour is more and more widely used. Whether you are looking for something traditional or something new, the cakes illustrated here should meet your needs, though you can of course make many of them either larger or smaller, or with more or fewer tiers.

As a rule, a multi-tier cake should taper smoothly from top to bottom. There are exceptions to this, as you will see, but by and large your proportions should be on the following lines:

For a 3-tier cake, make 3 cakes of 6in (15cm), 8in (20cm) and 10in (25cm), or in those proportions. The drums to match those measurements should be 8in (20cm), 10in (25cm) and 12in (30cm).

DREAMING ROSE

For many years red roses have been a symbol of love – a theme strikingly captured in this easy-to-decorate 3-tier hexagonal cake.

1 Place the cakes on round drums and Royal-ice.
2 Use No 16 Tube to pipe shells around both top and bottom edges, and No 14 Tube diagonally on sides.
3 Pipe lacework on the side of each tier, as illustrated, with No 1 Tube.
4 Fix on gum paste leaves, sprays and doves.
5 Attach white Decorette ribbon around the side of each drum.
6 Place pillars in position, tier the cakes and complete with Vase.

DECORATIONS

WON 108	Silver Vase, Red & Pink Bouquet ·
S 6125	Orchid & Rose Sprays (2)
F5395RE	Red Rosebuds (54)
PP 3230	Silver Pillars (8)
C 17	Leaves (18)
CP 1010	Doves (6)
CP 1011	Doves (12)
	Round Drums (3)
V 5279WH	White Decorette Ribbon

ICING TUBES

V 5125	Plain Tube No 1
V 5083	Rope Tube No 14
V 5084	Rope Tube No 16

☆ The use of round drums with a hexagonal cake shows that unusual shapes can still look attractive on standard drums.

DIANA

Tall and very pretty, this 3-tier hexagonal cake is one for the connoisseur with its flowing lines, fine detail and attractively contrasting colours of silver and pink. The unusual application of delicate lace banding is another noteworthy feature. This cake will more than repay the time taken to decorate it.

1 Having made and marzipanned the cakes, coat each tier in Royal Icing at least 3 times until flat and smooth.

2 When dry, mark the sides and top of each tier as illustrated, and overpipe the design. Make and use a template to ensure that each side is evenly decorated.

3 Place silver banding down each corner and around the drums, as illustrated.

4 Use No 16 Tube to pipe shells around the top and bottom edges of each tier. Overpipe shells with S scroll using Nos 3 and 2 tubes.

5 With a No 1 Tube and pink Royal Icing, overpipe all linework as illustrated.

6 Place on sprays and decorations, and allow to dry.

7 Add pillars, tier the cakes and complete with the Silver Basket top ornament.

DECORATIONS

WON 111	Silver Basket, Pink Spray
S 6110PI	Pink Treble Roses (6)
S 6109PI	Pink Double Roses (6)
S 6108PI	Single Roses (6)
PL 1401	Double Hearts (18)
PL 1402	Lovers' Knots (18)
PP 3230	Round Pillars (8)
BND 63	Silver Banding
	Hexagonal Drums (3)

ICING TUBES

V 5125	Plain Tube No 1
V 5074	Plain Tube No 2
V 5075	Plain Tube No 3
V 5084	Rope Tube No 16

BUTTERFLY

'Something old, something new, something borrowed, something blue.' This old tradition is at least partly fulfilled by the delicate blue butterflies which are complemented by the fine blue centres of the star flowers.

1 Coat cakes and tops of drums with white Royal Icing.
2 Using Star Tube No 31, pipe S shaped scrolls around the top and bottom edges.
3 Pipe diagonal rows of star flowers around the sides of the cakes.
4 Pipe a circle of stars around the top of each cake.
5 Using the No 1 Tube and blue coloured Royal Icing, pipe a small dot in the centre of all stars.
6 Fix banding around drums, add butterflies and pillars.
7 Tier the cakes and complete with the Silver Vase top ornament, adding 2 butterflies as a final touch.

DECORATIONS

BV 5149	Butterflies (26)
WON 32WH	Silver Vase Top Ornament
BND 63	Silver Banding
PP 3235	Round Pillars (8)
	Round Drums (3)

ICING TUBES

V 5125	Plain Tube No 1
V 5082	Star Tube No 31

☆ This bold icing is not difficult, and will help decorate the cake quickly.

When using Royal Icing, check that there is no grease on any of the utensils as this will spoil the icing.

Decorate a simple fan with flowers and a bow to make an interesting Wedding Day accessory.

FLORIDA

The unusual tiering arrangement of this 3-tier round cake is often seen in America. When combined with the cascade of flowers, the effect is especially attractive.

1 Having made and marzipanned your cakes, place the small and large cakes on normal-sized drums and the medium cake on thin card the same size as the cake will be after icing with Royal Icing.

2 Coat all cakes as usual and allow to dry.

3 Place the medium cake on the centre of the large cake.

4 Use No 44 Tube to pipe small scrolls on the top and bottom edges of all tiers (this will also join the large and medium cakes together). Pipe one scroll to the left and one to the right with a shell drawn down the side of the cake, joining the two scrolls together.

5 Overpipe scrolls on the top and bottom edges with Plain Tube No 4.

6 In pink coloured icing and with the No 44 Tube, pipe the ring of scrolls on the tops of both middle and top tiers.

7 Attach flowers to cakes, ensuring that a flowing curve is achieved on the opposite sides of the cake.

8 Add decorations and pillars, tier the top cake and complete with the Silver Vase top ornament.

DECORATIONS

F 5396PI	Pink Polyester Flowers (8)
F 5396WH	White Polyester Flowers (8)
S 6113PI	Pink Flowers & 2 Leaves (20)
WV 4484PI	Pink Heather (18)
WV 4484WH	White Heather (18)
S 54	White Lilies & Leaves (16)
CP 1033	Bell in Horseshoe
CP 1011	Doves (6)
PP 3235	Silver Pillars (4)
WON 794	Silver Vase Top Ornament
BND 63	Silver Banding
	Round Drums (2)
	Round Cake Card

ICING TUBES

V 5127	Rope Tube No 44
V 5076	Plain Tube No 4

☆ The piping is not difficult but the flowers need to be arranged with care. Either sugar or wafer roses may be used as an alternative.

BND 63	Silver Banding
P 4130	Hexagonal Pillars (6)
	Heart Drums (3)

ICING TUBES

V 5125	Plain Tube No 1
V 5074	Plain Tube No 2
V 5127	Rope Tube No 44

SWAN LAKE

The swan pillars and unusual wedding ornament combine to make this a superbly elegant cake.

1 Coat cakes and tops of drums with Royal Icing.
2 Pipe a twisted rope edging around the top edges of the cakes with an inner edging of small shells.
3 Pipe shells around the bottom edges, using No 44 Tube.
4 The doves around the sides of the cakes are piped separately. First draw a template of doves and cover with waxed paper. Pipe the bottom wing first and allow to dry. Then pipe the second wing and body using a No 1 Tube for all stages. Allow to dry and fix on cake.
5 Use the No 1 Tube to pipe curved lines joining the doves together.
6 Pipe small sugar bells where the curved lines meet.
7 Pipe linework on top of the cakes using Nos 3, 2 & 1 Tubes.
8 Add decorations as illustrated.

DECORATIONS

WON 793	Bride & Groom
CP 1072	Silver Horseshoes (12)
CP 1089	Silver Horseshoes (12)
WV 4609	Silver Slippers (4)
CP 1026	Dove on Silver Ring
PP 3333	Swan Pillars (8)
S 6131	Slippers & Blossom (4)
S 6106	Flower & Leaves (4)
S 6107	Flowers & Leaves (8)
BND 63	Silver Banding
	Round Drums (3)

ICING TUBES

V 5125	Plain Tube No 1
V 5074	Plain Tube No 2
V 5075	Plain Tube No 3
V 5127	Rope Tube No 44

☆ This cake uses oversize drums decorated with simple sprays. The piping is quite difficult and needs care to ensure that it is even, neat and tidy.

HEARTS AND BELLS

This 3-tier heart-shaped cake is one of several to meet the increasing demand for different shapes.

1 Coat cakes in Royal Icing and allow to dry.
2 Make a template of the design and mark lightly on each cake.
3 Pipe shells on top and bottom edges of cakes with No 44 Tube.
4 Using No 2 Tube, pipe the design on the sides and tops of the cakes.
5 With the illustration as your guide, pipe leaves with the Petal Tube, and with pink Royal Icing and No 1 Tube pipe the flowers.
6 Add bells, horseshoes and flower sprays.
7 Place on pillars, tier the cakes and complete with the Vase top ornament.

DECORATIONS

WON 114	White Vase Top Ornament
CP 1032	Double Bells (12)
CP 1072	Silver Horseshoes (4)
CP 1089	Silver Horseshoes (12)
BV 5027PI	Pink Satin Ribbon
S 6126	Flower Sprays (2)
S 6122	Blossom & Rose Leaves (3)

CONNEMARA

To some people green is unlucky but on this 3-tier cake the pale green icing has been used with outstanding effect.

1 Coat the cakes and drum tops in very pale green Royal Icing.
2 Pipe swirls around both top and bottom edges in slightly deeper green icing, using No 20 Tube.
3 Overpipe swirls with loops using No 3 Tube.
4 Divide and lightly mark each tier into 8 sections.
5 Pipe loops on the side of each cake between each section, as illustrated. Outline each double loop with a row of dots using No 1 Tube.
6 Use Nos 3 & 2 Tubes to pipe lines around the top surfaces of the cake, indenting the lines with a crescent shape between each section.
7 Overpipe the lines with Nos 2 & 1 Tubes and edge with a row of dots.
8 Pipe small doves freehand with No 1 Tube on the sides of the cakes.
9 Complete decoration and add vase.

DECORATIONS

S 6107	White Flowers (8)	
S 6106	White Flowers (4)	
S 274	Silver Slippers (12)	
S 273	Horseshoes (2)	
CP 1011	Doves (10)	
CP 1012	Doves (4)	
WV 4484WH	White Heathers (4)	
CP 1074	Silver Hearts (12)	
LS 1912	Silver Leaves (8)	
P 4130	Round Pillars (8)	
WON 32WH	Silver Vase Ornament	
	Round Drums (3)	

ICING TUBES

V 5125	Plain Tube No 1
V 5074	Plain Tube No 2
V 5075	Plain Tube No 3
V 5086	Rope Tube No 20

HARMONY

This 2-tier cake with silver horseshoes combines a British decorating style with a popular European fluting design on the sides of the cakes. It is not, by the way, as easy to decorate as it might at first appear, and is not recommended for the student.

1 Coat cakes with Royal Icing. Before sides of cake have dried, mark each into 3 sections and with a comb scraper draw horizontally across the outer sections, working outwards from the middle.
2 Pipe scrolls on top corners and overpipe with Nos 3, 2 & 1 Tubes in that order.
3 Pipe stars around bases and overpipe with loops using a No1 Tube.
4 Pipe linework on top surfaces, as illustrated, with No 1 Tube.

5 Fix sprays and horseshoes on cake, add pillars, tier cakes and add Bride & Groom top ornament.

DECORATIONS

WVS 4527	Silver Horseshoes (8)
CP 1027	Dove on Gold Ring
S 6110WH	Treble Roses (4)
S 6109WH	Double Roses (4)
P 4530	Square Plaster Pillars (4)
F 5395WH	White Rosebuds (4)
L 301	Leaves (16)
WON 700	Bride & Groom Ornament
	Square Drums (2)

ICING TUBES

V 5125	Plain Tube No 1
V 5074	Plain Tube No 2
V 5075	Plain Tube No 3
V 5127	Rope Tube No 44

SIMPLICITY

As the name implies, this is not an elaborate cake but the lace panels, coupled with the pink spray and ornament, lend it a special appeal.

1 Coat cakes and drums in white Royal Icing.
2 Using Leaf Tube No 66, pipe a pleated ribbon around the top edges and diagonally on the sides, as illustrated.
3 With No 0 Tube, pipe lacework in triangular shapes on the sides of the cakes.
4 Pipe stars around the base of each cake with No 18 Tube.
5 Use No 2 Tube to pipe broken lines around the edges of pleated ribbon.
6 Fix a silver band around the side of each cake drum and pipe a wavy line on the top edge of each drum.

7 Add decorations, tier the cakes and top with the Horseshoe ornament.

DECORATIONS

F 5395PI	Pink Rosebuds (8)
L 301	Leaves (8)
WON 105	Horseshoe & Pink Spray Top Ornament
CP 1051	Silver Bows (8)
WV 4609	Silver Slippers (8)
BND 63	Silver Banding
PP 6230	Silver Square Pillars (4)
	Square Drums (2)

ICING TUBES

V 5124	Plain Tube No 0
V 5074	Plain Tube No 2
V 5085	Plain Tube No 18
V 5092	Leaf Tube No 66

VICTORIA

This style of wedding cake was popular in the days of Queen Victoria, though the icing would have been white. Here the pastel shade enhances the white of the decorations and gives the cake a more modern appeal.

1 Having made and marzipanned your cake, coat as usual in pale yellow Royal Icing.
2 Pipe garlands on top and bottom edges, using Rope Tube No 44.
3 Overpipe garlands with Rope Tube No 43 and once more with No 2 Tube.
4 Position gum paste leaves using Royal Icing to fix.
5 Add spray and other decorations and allow to dry.
6 Place on pillars, tier the cake and complete with Vase top ornament.

DECORATIONS

WON 112	Vase Top Ornament
CP 1023	Doves on Silver Horseshoe (8)
C 40	Leaves (8)
C 19	Leaves (8)
S 6109WH	White Double Roses (6)
S 6108WH	White Single Roses (4)
P 6230	Square Silver Pillars (4)
	Square Drums (2)

ICING TUBES

V 5074	Plain Tube No 2
V 5126	Rope Tube No 43
V 5127	Rope Tube No 44

When the wedding is over, where do you put that ornament which was so special to you? Why not convert it into an attractive wall hanging or table centrepiece?

When assessing the size of cake you will require, a good guideline is to allow 1 sq in (6.5cm^2) per person.

ELIZABETH

The use of gold on this 2-tier wedding cake imparts a rich royal feeling.

1 Make square cakes and cut off corners, marzipan and coat cake and drum in pale yellow Royal Icing.
2 Pipe garlands on both top and bottom edges with No 44 Tube.
3 Overpipe garlands with Petal Tube, shaking the bag gently to obtain a wavy edge.
4 Using Nos 3, 2 & 1 Tubes, in that order, pipe all linework as illustrated.
5 Pipe lacework in the corners and in the centre of the top tier, using No 1 Tube.
6 With the No 1 Tube and a deeper shade of yellow Royal Icing, overpipe garlands on linework as illustrated.
7 Attach banding around sides and place on sprays, horseshoes and doves.
8 Place pillars in position, tier the cakes and complete with Vase top ornament.

DECORATIONS

WON 107	Gold Vase, Gold Spray
CP 1090	Gold Horseshoes (8)
CP 1027	Doves on Gold Rings (4)
S 6025	Gold Sprays (8)
PP 9130	Gold Pillars (4)
BND 62	Gold Banding
	Square Gold Drums (2)

ICING TUBES

V 5125	Plain Tube No 1
V 5074	Plain Tube No 2
V 5075	Plain Tube No 3
V 5088	Petal Tube No 61
V 5127	Rope Tube No 44

☆ The interesting way the corners have been shaped and decorated could be applied to other square cakes.

Use one of the special flowers to turn a summer hat into an Easter bonnet.

CELEBRATION

Attractive and easy to decorate, this cake is suitable for weddings and for many other occasions.

1 Cover cake and top of drum in Royal Icing.
2 Using a template, lightly mark the design on the sides and top of the cake.
3 Pipe shells with No 44 Tube around the top and bottom edges.
4 With No 2 Tube, pipe dots on top and sides of cake, as illustrated, ensuring that the dots are piped within the marked shape.

5 Fasten silver banding around drum and place on silver hearts and sprays to complete.

DECORATIONS

CP 1074	Silver Hearts (16)	
S 6118	Flower Rings (8)	
BND 65	Silver Banding	
	Square Drum	

ICING TUBES

V 5074	Plain Tube No 2	
V 5127	Rope Tube No 44	

☆ The illustration also features a Square Cake Stand (WV 5186).

Royal Icing, when not being used, should be covered with a damp cloth. It is advisable also to place a plastic bag over the basin and cloth to prevent drying out.

PINK PERFECTION

This traditional 3-tier square cake is easy to decorate and to adapt to other colour schemes of your choice.

1 Having made your cake, coat each tier and the top of each drum with white Royal Icing, and pipe shells using No 44 Tube.
2 With No 1 Tube, pipe lacework on the sides and top surfaces of the cake and on the top of the drum.
3 Pipe swirls around the top borders, and overpipe with Rope Tube No 43 in a crescent shape.
4 Fix on sprays and silver plastic wedding decorations, place pillars in position, tier the cakes and complete with Bride & Groom top ornament.

DECORATIONS

WVS 4527	Silver Horseshoes (4)
CP 1032	Double Bells (4)
CP 1034	Wishbones (4)
S 6110PI	Treble Roses (4)
S 6109PI	Double Roses (4)
S 6108PI	Single Roses (4)
WON 120	Bride & Groom on White Base
P 4530	Square Plastic Pillars (8)
F 5401PI	Blossom (4)
	Square Drums (3)
	$\frac{1}{2}$in (1.2cm) Pink Ribbon

ICING TUBES

V 5125	Plain Tube No 1
V 5126	Rope Tube No 43
V 5127	Rope Tube No 44

To make coloured icing successfully, always add colour gradually to icing.

GOOD LUCK

This cake is sure to be a winner with its lucky horseshoes theme!

1 Coat the cakes and tops of drums in Royal Icing.
2 Pipe a garland in the middle of both top and bottom edges, using Star Tube No 25.
3 Also with the Star Tube, pipe shells around the remaining edges.
4 Overpipe the garland with a loop using the Rope Tube No 20 and overpipe again with the Petal Tube No 61, shaking slightly to give a wavy edge.
5 Pipe lacework on the centre of each tier with No 2 Tube.
6 Fasten a silver band around the sides of each cake and drum. Fix on ribbon and all decorations.
7 Complete by placing on pillars, tiering cakes and adding Horseshoe top ornament.

DECORATIONS

WVS 4540	Horseshoes (20)	
PL 781	Bells (24)	
WON 787	Horseshoe Top Ornament	
PP 6235	Square Pillars (8)	
BND 65	Silver Banding	
	$\frac{1}{2}$in (1.2cm) Pink Ribbon	
	Square Drums (3)	

ICING TUBES

V 5074	Plain Tube No 2
V 5079	Star Tube No 25
V 5086	Rope Tube No 20
V 5088	Petal Tube No 61

An attractive table decoration can easily be made using a Silver Pillar (PP 3230) and Flower Ring (S 6118) with a candle placed in the top.

HAPPINESS

Horseshoe cakes are becoming popular once again and in this fine 3-tier example it is not difficult to see why. Note also how a basically white cake is lifted by the pastel-coloured ornament.

1 Make your cakes and coat them.
2 Pipe shells with No 44 Tube around the top and bottom edges.
3 Using No 2 Tube, pipe loops on either side of the shells on the top edge.
4 With No 1 Tube, overpipe with pale lilac icing.
5 Fix silver banding around the cakes and drums.
6 Place on horseshoes, sprays and pillars, tier the cakes and complete with the Silver Basket top ornament.

DECORATIONS

WON 110	Silver Basket, Lilac Spray
CP 1032	Double Bells (6)
CP 1034	Wishbones (6)
CP 1089	Horseshoes (12)
S 6121	Blossom (12)
PP 3130	Round Pillars (6)
BND 63	Silver Banding
BND 65	Silver Banding
	Horseshoe Drums (3)

ICING TUBES

V 5125	Plain Tube No 1
V 5074	Plain Tube No 2
V 5127	Rope Tube No 44

☆ Make sure your tins and drums are the same shape.

BRISBANE (see opposite).

We recommend using pillars with supports on all tiered cakes not made with heavy fruit cake and Royal Icing.

BRISBANE
The smooth Australian style of cake decorating is well represented here.

1 Having marzipanned the cakes, cover in Plastic Icing; allow to dry.
2 Pipe lacework on wax paper with No 1 Tube and allow to dry.
3 Pipe shallow loops with the Petal Tube around the sides of the cakes.
4 Mark a line around the cakes 1in (2.5cm) above loops, and with No 1 Tube pipe vertical lines.
5 With No 1 Tube, pipe dots to cover up joins.
6 Attach ribbon and pipe floral design and extra loops.
7 Add decorations and pillars, tier cakes and put on Bride & Groom.

DECORATIONS
WON 786	Bride & Groom
F 5395WH	White Rosebuds (16)
F 5395BL	Blue Rosebuds (10)
PP 3130	Round Pillars (4)
L 21	Leaves (15)
WV 4486	Lily of the Valley (16)
CP 1027	Dove on Gold Ring
	Round Drums (2)

ICING TUBES
V 5125	Plain Tube No 1
V 5088	Petal Tube No 61

PERTH
An unusual Australian design with small off-centre top tier.

1 Cover cakes in Plastic Icing and place on drums.
2 Roll out a length of Plastic Icing and place around bottom of cakes.
3 Fix to edge, crimp with tweezers.
4 To fix the ribbon, make vertical slits and insert carefully. Using the Rope Tube, pipe mini-shells of Royal Icing around the ribbon and each base.
5 Place pillars on the bottom tier and the main ornament on the top tier. Pipe small stars around these.
6 Fix banding around the drums, place on sprays and dove.
7 Tier the cake to complete.

DECORATIONS
WON 119	Heart & Roses
CP 1026	Doves on Rings (2)
S 6112PI	Pink Blossom (7)
PP 3130	Round Pillars (4)
F 5395PI	Pink Rosebuds (12)
L 301	Leaves (12)
BV 5027PI	Pink Ribbon
BND 63	Silver Banding
	Square Drums (2)

ICING TUBES
V 5126	Rope Tube No 43

Why is it that proper birthday cakes tend to stop when childhood is over? Here we have designs for young and old!

SARAH

A sophisticated L-shaped cake for a young lady's coming of age.

1 Make the cake square with one quarter cut out.
2 Marzipan and cover with Plastic Icing and place on the drum.
3 Pipe shells with No 44 Tube.
4 Using No 3 Tube, pipe flowers.
5 Pipe leaves on the flowers in pale green Royal Icing; use No 2 Tube.
6 Complete by adding decorations.

DECORATIONS

PX 1150	Crinoline Lady with Hat
S 6103PI	18th Birthday Spray
F 5396PI	Polyester Flowers (6)
CP 1056	Congratulations Motto
BV 4584PI	Candles (18)
CH 2PI	Candle Holders (18)
S 6112PI	Blossom (5)
BV 5027PI	Ribbon
	Square Drum

ICING TUBES

V 5074	Plain Tube No 2
V 5075	Plain Tube No 3
V 5127	Rope Tube No 44

DAISY

The unusual combination of sugar flowers and moulded sugar leaves give this square 18th Birthday cake an attractive and appealing look.

1 Coat the cake with Royal Icing, place it on a drum and ice the drum.
2 Place 2 sugar flowers on each corner and one in the middle.
3 Pipe shells with No 44 Tube around the base of the cake and between the sugar flowers on the top edges.
4 With No 2 Tube, overpipe the shells and outline top of cake.
5 Place a silver band around sides and fix on all sugar paste leaves.
6 Outline the sugar paste leaves in the middle of the cake and pipe a scalloped line around the outside top edge of the drum.
7 Complete by adding the 18th Key.

DECORATIONS

SF 161	Sugar Flowers (9)
C 17	Sugar Paste Leaves (4)
C 18	Sugar Paste Leaves (4)
CP 1060	18th Silver Key
BND 63	Silver Banding
	Square Drum

ICING TUBES

V 5074	Plain Tube No 2
V 5127	Rope Tube No 44

CONTESSA

One of the most frequently requested birthday cakes – by girls of all ages.

1 Make the cake in a pudding basin.
2 Cover in pale pink Sugar Paste and attach Crinoline Lady.
3 Roll out pale blue Sugar Paste and cover the area of the skirt, apart from the front panel, as illustrated.
4 With white Royal Icing and a Leaf Tube, pipe ruffles down the edge of the panel, and pipe three rows of ruffles around the base of the cake.
5 Using No 1 Tube, pipe minute dot flowers on the panel of the dress.
6 With the Leaf Tube, pipe ribbon scallops around lower part of dress.
7 Now use Rope Tube to pipe star flowers on the Crinoline Lady.
8 Complete with ribbon bows, wafer roses and motto.

DECORATIONS

PX 1162	Crinoline Lady
BV 5027WH	White Satin Ribbon
WE 20	Small Wafer Roses (21)
PL 1208	Happy Birthday Motto
	Round Drum

ICING TUBES

V 5125	Plain Tube No 1
V 5085	Rope Tube No 18
V 5092	Leaf Tube No 66

ROSE

Quick and easy to decorate, this hexagonal cake would delight any young lady.

1 Cover cake with Sugar Paste and place on drum.
2 Pipe a shell edge with Royal Icing around the base.
3 Add the decorations to complete.

DECORATIONS

BV 5027PI	Pink Ribbon
WE 21	Wafer Roses (12)
BV 4632	Ballet Dancers (7)
L 301	Silver Leaves (18)
CH 2PI	Candle Holders (as required)
ST 2344	Candles (as required)
PL 1208	Happy Birthday Motto
	Round Drum

ICING TUBE

V 5080	Star Tube No 27

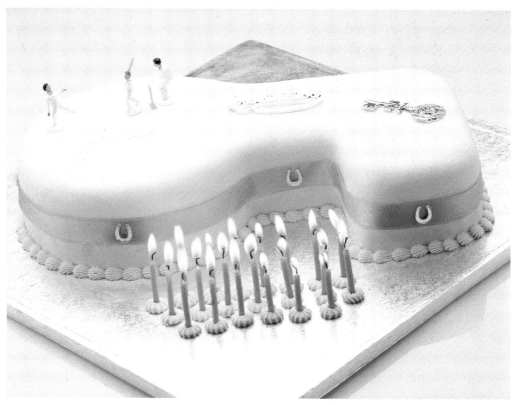

SPORT

If cricket is not their game, this 21st Key cake is adaptable to many other sports.

1 Bake a fruit cake in a key-shaped tin. Alternatively, bake one round cake and one square, and cut and join
2 Cover with marzipan and Sugar Paste and place on drum.
3 In pale blue Royal Icing, using No 44 Tube, pipe shells around the base.
4 Place ribbon around the sides of the cake and stick on horseshoes.
5 Using No 44 Tube and blue Royal Icing, pipe 21 swirls on the drum; push a candle in the centre of each swirl.
6 With No 2 Tube, pipe the name on the cake.
7 Add Cricketers, Congratulations motto and 21st Key to complete.

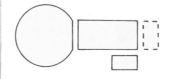

Make a rough sketch of the cake and any templates required.

DECORATIONS

PL 1357	Cricketers Set (1 batsman, 1 bowler, 1 wicket, 1 wicket-keeper)
CP 1072	Horseshoes (7)
CP 1056	Congratulations Motto
CP 1059	21st Silver Key
BV 5027BL	Blue Ribbon
BV 4584BL	Blue Candles (21)
CH 2BL	Blue Candle Holders (21)
	Square or Oblong Drum

ICING TUBES

V 5074	Plain Tube No 2
V 5127	Rope Tube No 44

☆ A safer alternative to the Royal Icing swirls holding the candles is to place them in candle holders (listed above).

GETTING THE SHAPE
Use round and rectangular cakes to make your key shape.

COMING OF AGE

The key – traditional symbol of adulthood attained – here makes a charming and delicately embellished cake.

1 Make a sponge in a key shape, place on a drum and cover in Butter Cream.
2 Coat the sides in chocolate sugar strands or any covering of your choice.
3 Using either chocolate or brown coloured Royal Icing, pipe the design as illustrated on top of cake.
4 Pipe the inscription and add flowers to complete.

DECORATIONS

S 6102PI	Pink 21st Spray
S 6118	Ring of Flowers
	Oblong Drum

ICING TUBE

V 5125	Plain Tube No 1

TEAM SPIRIT

1 Cover an oblong shaped cake in green coloured Sugar Paste.
2 Using marzipan tweezers, decorate the top edges of the cake.
3 With fine strips of white Sugar Paste, or white Royal Icing and Plain Tube No2, mark out the pitch.
4 Place on footballers and goal posts.
5 Colour some granulated sugar green and sprinkle over the top.
6 Roll out white Sugar Paste and cut into oblong plaques. Paint or pipe on with No1 Tube 'It's A Goal', the name and 'Happy Birthday'. When dry, fix to cake with Royal Icing.
7 Use Sugar Paste to cut out the age figure or use plastic numerals.
8 Place frill around sides, complete with centre ribbon and mascot.

DECORATIONS

BV 4754	Goalkeepers (2)
BV 4756	Assorted Footballers
BV 4755	Goalposts (2)
FR 1052	Blue Birthday Cake Frill 1in (2.5cm) Ribbon
PL 1292-1301	Plastic Numerals (optional)
	Oblong Drum

ICING TUBES

V 5125	Plain Tube No1
V 5074	Plain Tube No2

COPENHAGEN

A sophisticated design from a well-known Danish baker.
1 Layer and cover a sponge in Butter Cream.
2 Roll out marzipan to the desired shape and cover the cake.
3 Cut out the horseshoe shape, petals and plaque, and place the train on the cake.
4 Press candle holders through petals to fix on the cake. Pipe the child's name and age on the plaque, underlining the plaque with a scroll, using No 1 Tube.
5 Roll out more coloured marzipan patterning as required and place around the side of the cake.
6 Complete by inserting candles in the holders.

DECORATIONS

PL 885	Engine Candle Holder
PL 886	Carriage Candle Holders (as required)
CH 2	Candle Holders (as required)
BV 4584	Candles (as required)

ICING TUBE

V 5125	Plain Tube No 1

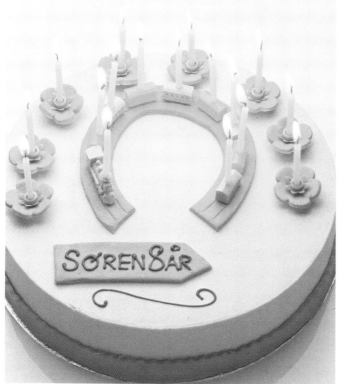

ENCHANTMENT

Whatever the age, this Crinoline Lady cake will charm any celebration.
Cake Size: Dolly Varden Tin.
(Alternatively, a pudding basin.)

1 Cover the cake with Sugar Paste and leave to harden.
2 Cut 1in (2.5cm) wide strips of sugar paste, crimp the outside edge with marzipan tweezers and fix on the cake, overlapping and pleating each layer as illustrated.
3 Cover the remainder of the cake with pink Sugar Paste.
4 Insert a ribbon round the edge (see page 23), and with Royal Icing pipe flowers between the ribbon inserts.
5 Position the lady, pipe scallops round her waist and sleeves and flowers on her hat.
6 Pipe small flowers and leaves randomly over the dress.
7 Add sprays and blossom as shown.

DECORATIONS

PX 1150	Crinoline Lady with Hat
S 3089	Blossom (2)
F 5395WH	White Rosebuds (12)
	$\frac{1}{2}$in (1.2cm) Pink Ribbon
	Round Drum

ICING TUBE

V 5125	Plain Tube No 1

SUNSHINE
Fine white filigree piping on a pale yellow base produces this classic cake from Australia, a country renowned for its sun.

1 Make a hexagonal cake, cover in Sugar Paste and place on drum.
2 Using a Rope Tube, pipe vertical elongated shells around the base of the cake.
3 From alternate top ends of the elongated shells, using a No 1 Tube, pipe loops around the cake and overpipe the join with small dots.
4 Pipe fine filigree work on wax paper and allow to dry thoroughly; remove from wax paper and fix on cake.

5 Place ribbon around the cake.
6 Pipe on dot flowers, as illustrated.
7 Complete by placing in position the sprays and key.

DECORATIONS

S 6025	Heather & Rose Gold Sprays (4)
CP 1085	21st Gold Key
	Yellow Ribbon
	Round Drum

ICING TUBES

V 5125	Plain Tube No 1
V 5127	Rope Tube No 44

☆ Change the decoration slightly and this can become a magnificent Golden Anniversary cake.

CAROUSEL

An easy cake, but lots of fun.

1 Make a round cake and cut off top.
2 Cover the top part of the cake with marzipan, and place on thin card the same diameter as the cake.
3 Cover the top of the base with marzipan and coat with Royal Icing.
4 Coat the top cake with Royal Icing and sprinkle on nonpareils.
5 Pipe a shell edging around the top of the base cake and the bottom of the top cake, using No 20 Tube.
6 The centre of the cake is made with half a Swiss roll covered with marzipan and Royal Icing; decorate with a comb scraper.
7 Cut plastic straws approx. 3in (8cm) long and press into the icing.
8 Place animal figures on centre of cake. Put the top in position and complete with motto and frill.

DECORATIONS

PL 1403	Animal Figures (12)
CP 1053	Silver Happy Birthday
FR 1052	Horses Frill
ST 2172	Nonpareils
	Thin Card
	Round Drum

ICING TUBES

V 5086	Rope Tube No 20

ROUNDABOUT

A light and creamy cake from Canada, best made and eaten on the day itself.

1 Make the cake and either a puff pastry or shortbread base of the same diameter, and cut this into sections. Place on drum.
2 Pipe fresh cream swirls on the top of the cake.
3 Place on the pastry sections. Pipe a swirl of cream in the middle.
4 Place a cake frill around the side and a Disney candle holder in every portion.

DECORATIONS

PL 1233	Assorted Disney Candle Holders (as required).
BV 4584	Candles (as required).
FR 1004	Happy Birthday Frill.
	Round Drum

ICING TUBE

TV 4873	Star Tube Size 9

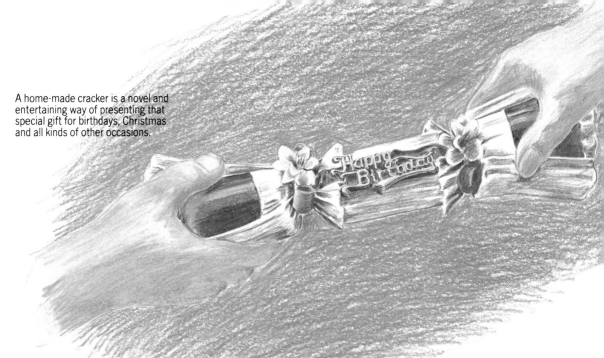

A home-made cracker is a novel and entertaining way of presenting that special gift for birthdays, Christmas and all kinds of other occasions.

CIRCUS RING

An amusing and novel birthday cake, this will bring a smile to the children's faces.

1 Make 2 sponge cakes and sandwich together with cream.
2 Cover the top and then the sides with one piece of Sugar Paste, and place on the drum.
3 Use a little Royal Icing to spread over the top and sprinkle on coloured coconut 'sawdust'.
4 Using red coloured Sugar Paste, roll out and then cut out a ring ½in (1.2cm) smaller than the diameter of the cake and approx. 1in (2.5cm) wide. Cut into 8 equal segments and leave to dry overnight.
5 Make a side plaque by cutting a strip of red coloured Sugar Paste approx. 7in (18cm) long and 1in (2.5cm) wide; attach to the side of the cake.
6 Roll out pink coloured Sugar Paste and cut out about 20 faces using a 1in (2.5cm) diameter cutter.
7 Pipe 'Happy Birthday' on the plaque and pipe or paint the faces with food colour.
8 Place the faces on the drum around the side of the cake.
9 Attach the red ring edges to the top of the cake and place a ½in (1.2cm) band around the side.
10 Complete by adding candles, holders and circus animals.

DECORATIONS

BV 5319	Assorted Circus Animals (5)	
BND 63	Silver Banding	
CH 2BL	Blue Candle Holders (as required)	
BV 4584BL	Blue Candles (as required)	
	Round Drum	

ICING TUBES

V 5074	Plain Tube No 2
V 5075	Plain Tube No 3
V 5080	Star Tube No 27

☆ An alternative to the faces is to use Circus Waferettes (WFL 119) and the HAPPY BIRTHDAY letters (PL 1399).

BIRTHDAY BOY

Children love numeral cakes.

1 Bake a sponge in a numeral tin, or make an oblong sponge and cut out. (Use the left-over sponge to make individual iced fancies.)
2 Cover with blue Sugar Paste and place on the drum.
3 Decorate the top with tweezers.
4 Place 2in (5cm) silver banding around the sides.
5 Pipe a shell edge around the top and bottom edges with No 20 Tube.
6 Place on the motor bikes, motto, candles and holders.

DECORATIONS

V 5213	Large Motor Bike	
PL 1313	Silver Motor Bikes (2)	
CP 1053	Silver Happy Birthday Motto	
CH 2WH	White Candle Holders	
ST 2344	Candles (as required)	
BND 69	Silver Banding	
	Round Drum	

ICING TUBE

V 5086	Rope Tube No 20

☆ By using pink Sugar Paste and different decorations, this could easily be changed into a cake for a girl.

BIG CHIEF

Whether he is a Big Chief or Little Brave, this Indian Village cake will delight all ages.

1 Make 2 cakes using large and small pudding basins, cover with Sugar Paste and place on a large drum.
2 Roll out Sugar Paste and cut out wigwam flaps (doors). Place on cakes as shown.
3 Colour cocktail sticks with food colour. Allow to dry and place in the tops of cakes.
4 Cover the drum with Royal Icing and sprinkle on maize meal and cocoa. As an alternative for maize meal, use crushed cornflakes.
5 Pipe patterns on the wigwams, as illustrated.
6 Complete by adding Cowboy and Indian figures and the Happy Birthday motto.

DECORATIONS

V 5220	Cowboys (as required)
V 5219	Indians (as required)
V 5218	Horse
PL 1315	Happy Birthday Motto
	Square Drum

ICING TUBE

V 5076	Plain Tube No 4

SPACE INVADERS

From the far beyond, a space ship arrives... bringing delight and fascination.

1 Make a large round cake and a small cake baked in a pudding shaped vessel.

2 Cover the round cake in Sugar Paste, leaving the top uneven and introducing craters by pressing a spoon or cone shaped utensil into the surface of the cake.

3 Roll Sugar Paste into small boulder shapes and place around top and bottom edges of cake: place randomly on top.

4 Using food colours, paint the boulders on the top of the cake to give a suitable effect. Sprinkle with extra granulated sugar to enhance this effect – while the surface is still moist.

5 Roll out a further ring of Sugar Paste approx. 1in (2.5cm) high and 3in (8cm) in diameter and place in the centre of the cake; allow to harden.

6 Place the pudding shaped cake on thin card which is at least 2in (5cm) larger in diameter than the cake.

7 Cover the cake and top of drum in light green Sugar Paste.

8 Using No 1 Tube and Royal Icing, pipe windows and all linework on the space ship, as illustrated.

9 Fill in windows and lights, etc, with either piping jelly or quick setting jelly. Alternatively, use brightly coloured Royal Icing in each section. The top of the cake should also be covered in the jelly.

10 The bands on the cake illustrated have been painted with silver food colouring; since this is not available or permitted in all countries, we suggest using an alternative colour to silver.

11 Place the small cake on the centre of the round cake, pipe on ladders with a No 1 Tube, place on space figures and complete by adding a frill around the sides of the large cake and using candles as antennae on the top.

DECORATIONS

V 5217	Assorted Space Figures (8)
BV 5336	Spacemen (2)
BV 4584	Candles
FR 644	Birthday Cake Frill
	Round Drum
	Round Thin Card

ICING TUBE

V 5125	Plain Tube No 1

ENCHANTED FAIRY CASTLE

From the land of dreams, a novel cake just right for any little Miss.

1 Make a square sponge cake and cut off each corner, using a 3in (8cm) diameter pastry cutter.
2 Cover the cake with Sugar Paste.
3 Take 2 Swiss rolls, cut each in half and cover with Sugar Paste.
4 Place the rolls as towers in the cut-out corners of the cake.
5 Using left-over cake from the corners, make a step and cover with Sugar Paste; place at the front of the castle.
6 Pipe shells with Star Tube around the edges including the vertical ones where the cake joins the towers. Overpipe shells with No 2 Tube.
7 Pipe on the child's name with No 1 Tube.
8 Place decorations on the cake and complete by adding spires made from the silver doilies. Cut each doily from the edge to the centre and make into a cone shape.

DECORATIONS

ST 2344	Candles (as required)
BV 4632	Ballet Dancers (5)
BV 5149	Butterflies (8)
CP 1053	Silver Happy Birthday Motto
ST 401	Pink/White Candle Holders (as required)
	Square Drum

ICING TUBES

V 5125	Plain Tube No 1
V 5074	Plain Tube No 2
V 5080	Star Tube No 27

SPELLBOUND

A fantasy castle for everyone. Just modify the decorations to match a favourite nursery rhyme or fairy story.

1 Make a firm sponge, e.g. Genoese, cut as shown in the diagram and assemble.
2 Cover with Sugar Paste.
3 Stick on sugar cubes for battlements.
4 Using brown Sugar Paste, cut out and fit door.
5 With No 2 Tube, pipe windows and flowers.
6 Cover the steps in Royal Icing and sprinkle on sugar strands.
7 Cover the drum in green Royal Icing and sprinkle on sugar strands.
8 Place on decorations, including spires (made as for the Enchanted Fairy Castle).

DECORATIONS

ST 2172	Sugar Strands
BV 4632	Ballet Dancers (2)
BV 5149	Butterflies (2)
BV 5320	Musical Gnomes (2)
BFC 22	Bo-Peep, 2 Sheep
ST 2171	Sugar Flowers

ICING TUBE

V 5074	Plain Tube No 2

WHIRLY BIRD

It may look difficult, but provided you get the basic shape correct this is a very simple cake.

1 Make a rectangular cake, draw a template of a helicopter shape and cut out. Place on cake and cut round outline.
2 Using red Sugar Paste, cut out rotor blades and leave to dry.
3 Cover drum in green Sugar Paste, marking the surface to give a patterned design.
4 Cover the helicopter in yellow Sugar Paste and place on drum.
5 Fix windows and rotor blades in position with Royal Icing.
6 Place on aircraft, Happy Birthday motto and numeral.

DECORATIONS

LA 79	Wafer Windows (12)
BV 5325	Assorted Aircraft (5)
PL 1297	Number 5 (or as required)
CP 1053	Silver Happy Birthday Motto
	Round Drum

☆ Don't forget the candles and candle holders – or just add a numeral candle to complete.

☆ On the facing page we show two designers' approach to the same subject. A third would perhaps have used the same base to produce a fort with Cowboys and Indians.

DONALD'S PARTY

This tribute to Walt Disney's characters was designed by a baker in Singapore – further proof of their universal appeal.

1 Cover the top only of the cake in marzipan, and when dry coat in Royal Icing.
2 Divide top of cake into 8 sections and, using No 2 Tube and brown coloured icing, pipe linework as featured.
3 Using pink icing and No 1 Tube, pipe fine linework with a looping action around the cake.
4 Use a large Star Tube to pipe swirls between each loop, and before the icing has a chance to dry place a Disney waferette on each swirl.
5 Place a Disney cake frill around the side of the cake.
6 Complete by adding figures, Disney candle holders, candles and Happy Birthday motto.

DECORATIONS

PL 1233	Disney Candle Holders (3)
BV 5330	Mickey Mouse
BV 5329	Minnie Mouse
BV 5327	Donald Duck
FR 925	Disney Frill
CP 1053	Happy Birthday Motto

ICING TUBES

V 5125	Plain Tube No 1
V 5074	Plain Tube No 2
V 5081	Star Tube No 29

BIRTHDAY CUP CAKE

Why does the birthday boy or girl have *all* the fun when it comes to blowing out the candles? Give the guests a chance with their own individual fancy cake – complete with candle – in addition to a slice of the main birthday cake.

GOLF COURSE CAKE

This could serve as a prize as well as a birthday cake.

1 Having made and marzipanned the cake, cover with green Royal Icing to produce an uneven, rolling surface like a golf course.
2 Mix a spot of green food colour with 1oz (30g) granulated sugar.
3 Sprinkle the green sugar on the icing when still wet. Do not cover completely, but leave the fairway areas uncovered to highlight them.
4 Using orange food colour, paint hollows to represent bunkers.
5 Make flags for bunkers using cocktail sticks and coloured self-adhesive labels.
6 Pipe shells around the top of the cake with No 20 Tube.
7 Place on figures and motto. Cover sides with frill.

DECORATIONS

BV 5322	Golfers (3)
PL 1315	Happy Birthday Motto
FR 1004	Happy Birthday Frill
	Round Drum

ICING TUBE

V 5086	Rope Tube No 20

☆ A green base can be used for most sporting cakes.

READY STEADY GO

Quick to make and decorate, this is a good effective cake for those with little time.

1 Make a round cake and marzipan the top surface only.
2 Coat the top in white Royal Icing.
3 Pipe a shell edge around the top side of the cake.
4 Place on motto, numeral and

candle holders and candles.
5 When the shell edge is dry, place a cake frill around the side of the cake.

DECORATIONS

PL 1315	Happy Birthday Motto
PL 1296	Number 4 (or as required)
FR 1052	Animal Frill
PL 1406	Animal Candle Holders (as required)
ST 2344	Candles (as required)
	Round Drum

ICING TUBE

V 5086	Rope Tube No 20

☆ The sporting animal sets are ideal for joggers, runners, cyclists, roller skaters, skiers and motorists – not forgetting pogo stick enthusiasts.

MAYPOLE CAKE

Donald Duck, Mickey Mouse and their friends never lose their appeal. This is an easy idea which will be popular with both boys and girls.
1 Coat cake in either Royal Icing or Sugar Paste.
2 Divide top of cake into sections and mark.
3 Pipe shells over marked lines with No 43 Tube and around top and bottom edges with No 44 Tube.
4 Place on decorations, using a plastic straw as a centre pole to hold the ribbons. When the cake is dry, place a frill around the side.

DECORATIONS

BV 5326	Mickey Mouse
BV 5327	Donald Duck (2)
BV 5328	Goofy
BV 5329	Minnie Mouse
BV 5330	Mickey Mouse & Ball
SF 420	Sugar Stars
WFL 20	Assorted Disney Waferettes (6)
FR 1052	Birthday Frill
	Round Drum

ICING TUBES

V 5126	Rope Tube No 43
V 5127	Rope Tube No 44

Never use a metal object to clean or unblock a piping tube as this will cause damage to the tube. After use, soak tube in water until icing is soft, then wash out.

Christmas is a time for families to get together, and cakes have long been a tradition at family gatherings. Tastes, however, are changing in the UK, moving away from the fruit cake and more to the lighter type of gateau or chocolate log. Of course, a lot of families have both!

For all that, cake decorations remain firmly traditional, and Father Christmas is by far the most popular character on Christmas cakes. Don't forget that many Christmas cake decorations are also useful for decorating the house, the table, or that special Christmas card or present.

INDIVIDUAL CHRISTMAS CRACKERS

Edible table decorations, based on mini Swiss rolls, that are fun and easy to make.

1 Roll out Sugar Paste to about twice the length of each mini Swiss roll and wide enough to go round it.
2 Cover roll and pinch in the Paste at each end, as illustrated. Place on log card.
3 Roll out red Sugar Paste, cut thin strips and place on cracker.
4 Using a fork, press into ends of crackers to give a patterned effect.
5 Complete by placing a decoration on the middle of the cracker.

DECORATIONS

ST 2276	These decorations, although
ST 2230	not in the Catalogue, are widely available in retail shops at Christmas.
	Log Card

CHRISTMAS PARCEL CAKE

This was a second designer's answer. All the decorations on this attractive teatime centrepiece are edible.

1 Cover cake in Sugar Paste.
2 Roll out red coloured Sugar Paste and cut into 1in (2.5cm) strips long enough to go across the cake. Make a bow and place in the centre.
3 Add the Christmas waferetttes and complete with wafer motto.

DECORATIONS

WFL 119	Waferettes (100)
EMB 942	Oblong Wafer Motto
	Square Drum

☆ Either of the Parcel cakes on these pages can be converted to a Birthday cake simply by changing the decorations.

HOLLY PARCEL CAKE

This is one designer's delightful solution to decorating a box-shaped Christmas cake.

1 Cover cake in Royal Icing until flat and smooth. Allow to dry and place on drum.
2 Place red coloured ribbon on the cake, as illustrated, and make a ribbon bow and fix to the centre.
3 Make a label from Sugar Paste; allow to dry before putting in position.
4 Add pieces of holly, bells and motto.

DECORATIONS

HP 1533	Holly Leaves (108 here; less if desired)
BV 5027	Red Ribbon
PL 1400	Large Bells (2)
PL 909	Gold Merry Christmas Motto
	Square Drum

CRACKER CAKE

An amusing way of presenting a light Swiss roll to your Christmas guests.

1 Cover Swiss roll in red coloured Sugar Paste.
2 Roll out paste, and using a glass or similar vessel of the same diameter as the Swiss roll, draw paste around sides of glass until smooth and approx. 2in (5cm) high. Cut off excess paste to leave a level edge; to ensure paste does not stick to glass, first dust with cornflour.
3 When part dry, remove glass and with a sharp knife or scissors cut a frill around the top edge approx. 1in (2.5cm) deep. Repeat Stages 2 and 3 to make 2 ends.
4 Place Swiss roll on the middle of an oblong card; add the ends to the body of the cracker.
5 Fasten ½in (1.2cm) banding around each end of the body of the cracker.
6 Dab white Royal Icing on to cracker; place on decorations as illustrated.

DECORATIONS

F 5396	White Flowers (3)
PL 909	Merry Christmas Motto
ST 1160	Assorted Holly and Mistletoe
BND 63	Banding
	Oblong Card

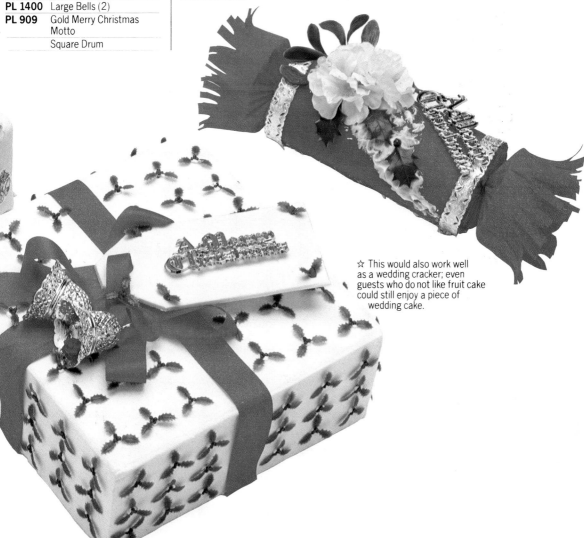

☆ This would also work well as a wedding cracker; even guests who do not like fruit cake could still enjoy a piece of wedding cake.

CHRISTMAS POST BOX
A novel reminder of one of the great annual customs – the giving and receiving of Christmas cards – and presents, too, of course!

1 Cover the side of a large Swiss roll in red Sugar Paste and allow to dry.
2 Place a strip of black coloured Sugar Paste approx. 1in (2.5cm) wide around the Swiss roll, as illustrated.
3 Place the Swiss roll upright on a drum which has been Royal-iced to give a snow effect.
4 The top of the pillar box is made by rolling out black Sugar Paste to a diameter slightly larger than that of the roll, and forming the top into a convex shape.
5 Cut out an oblong strip of black Paste for the letter box opening and a white square for the door; attach these to the side of the box.
6 Dab Royal Icing on the top of the box, as shown, and complete by adding the decorations.

DECORATIONS

H 9	Holly (2)
PL 909	Gold Merry Christmas Motto
PL 601	Light Brown Robins (2)
	Round Drum

SNOWBOYS
This Christmas cake is really quick, easy and fun to make.

1 Cover the cake with Sugar Paste and place on drum.
2 Put a small amount of Royal Icing on top of the cake, as illustrated, and cover the top surface of the drum.
3 Place holly around the top side of the cake, the ski figures on the drum and complete by adding Father Christmas and the signpost on top.

DECORATIONS

HP 1533	Holly Leaves (16)
PL 837	Father Christmas on Skis
PL 763	Signpost
PL 1282	Assorted Snowboys (10)
	Round Drum

PLUM PUDDING CAKE

An interesting alternative to the traditional Christmas cake.

1 Make the cake in a basin and cover with brown coloured Sugar Paste. Place on drum.
2 Roll out white Sugar Paste approx. 6in (15cm) wide, giving it a wavy edge as shown, and place on cake.
3 Paint fruit on the brown Sugar Paste using food colours.
4 Complete by topping with Christmas spray.

DECORATIONS

HP 1919	Merry Christmas Motto on Holly
	Round Drum

HERE COMES SANTA

Another easy fun cake that doesn't even need an icing tube.

1 Make a square cake, cut as shown in the diagram and marzipan.
2 Place cake on drum and cover with Sugar Paste.
3 Place decorations on cake and complete by adding gold banding around the edge of the drum.

DECORATIONS

PL 837	Father Christmas on Skis
PL 765	House
CV 5333	Green Trees (5)
PL 1264	Happy Christmas Motto
HP 1532	Holly Leaves (2)
BND 62	Gold Banding
	Square Drum

> When using coloured icing, be sure to make enough in the initial mix, as it is very difficult to achieve a colour match with a second batch.

LANTERN CAKE

The warm glow of Christmas is captured in this attractive novelty cake.

1 Make the cake and cut out a lantern shape.
2 Cover with marzipan and then with brown coloured Sugar Paste. Place on drum.
3 Roll out yellow coloured Sugar Paste and cut to shape as illustrated; place on cake.
4 Roll out red coloured Sugar Paste and cut out a candle and flame and place on cake.
5 Cut 2 oblong strips in brown Sugar Paste and place on cake as shown.
6 Using Royal Icing, cover the top of the lantern to give a snow effect.
7 Repeat this effect in a small band across the cake just below the candle.
8 Pipe shells around the bottom edge with No 44 Tube.
9 Add the motto, holly spray and figures to the cake.
10 Use Royal Icing to ice the snow scenes on the drum, and add the figures and trees.

DECORATIONS

CV 5334	Silver Trees (3)
CV 5335	Gold Trees (3)
CV 5332	Assorted Children (6)
PL 1265	Happy Christmas Motto, with Robin & Lantern
HP 2032	Holly Spray
	Square Drum

ICING TUBE

V 5127	Rope Tube No 44

CHRISTMAS LOGS

This style of cake is popular throughout Europe, and with a logpile that big there should be plenty for everyone.

1 Make 2 Swiss rolls and cut as shown in the diagram.
2 Cover the drum in white Royal Icing and place the Swiss roll in position.
3 Cover the Swiss roll in chocolate Butter Cream using a fork to make a bark effect.
4 Place log ends on each end, as shown.
5 Here and there, add Royal Icing 'snow' to the logs.
6 Complete by adding the decorations.

DECORATIONS

PL 1026	Axe
PL 601	Light Brown Robin
H 2249	Red & Gold Holly Sprays (2)
H 2217	Gold & Green Holly with Roses (2)
LA 72	Log Ends (3)
CV 5331	Christmas Animal Figure
BND 62	Gold Banding
	Round Drum

HANSEL AND GRETEL GINGERBREAD HOUSE

A traditional European celebration cake which is both appealing and distinctive. Although not quick to produce, it is easier to make than it may look.

1 Make a cardboard template of a gingerbread house. Roll out gingerbread dough, cut to shape of template and bake.
2 When cool, trim gingerbread to shape, cover cake drum in white Royal Icing and stand the walls of the gingerbread house on drum, fixing with Royal Icing.
3 Place roof on, fixing with Royal Icing, and tile it with chocolate drops.
4 Use chocolate finger biscuits to make the chimney.
5 Place orange and lemon slices along the top of the roof.
6 Place windows and doors in position, and sweets on the sides of the cake as illustrated.
7 Place sweets and decorations on the drum.
8 Complete by piping icicles on the roof, dust with icing sugar and add robin to chimney.

DECORATIONS

PL 784	Father Christmas on Sledge
PL 600	Dark Brown Robin
LA 79	Windows (2)
LA 80	Door
PX 27	Small Snowmen (2)
TNP 15	Trees (3)
	Square Drum
	Variety of Sweets

ICING TUBE

V 5074	Plain Tube No 2

☆ Change the decorations and this could easily be made into a Birthday cake.

FATHER CHRISTMAS ON SKATES

A clever use of rough icing combined with good design make a very smart Christmas cake.

1 Place the cake on the drum and cover with white Royal Icing. Make the top surface flat, and use a comb on the side to produce the pattern illustrated.
2 Add extra icing around the top edge to enhance the snow effect.
3 Using No 3 Tube, pipe large dots around the top and bottom edges of the cake.
4 With No 1 Tube and red coloured Royal Icing, pipe small dots between the large dots.
5 Complete by adding trees and figures to the top of the cake and holly to the side.

DECORATIONS

V 5225	Father Christmas Skating
PX 27	Snowmen (3)
HP 1531	Holly Leaves (3)
PL 875	Green Trees (3)
	Round Drum

ICING TUBES

V 5125	Plain Tube No 1
V 5075	Plain Tube No 3

TRADITIONAL CAKE

The appearance of a cake can be altered by repositioning , or using an unusual shape or size drum.

1 Place the marzipanned cake off-centre on the drum and Royal-ice the cake and drum until they are flat and smooth.
2 Add extra icing to the back part of the top of the cake and roughen it to simulate snow.
3 Pipe shells around top and bottom edges of the cake and on the outer edge of the drum, using No 14 Tube.
4 Place on Christmas figures, motto and holly and allow to dry.
5 Complete by fixing gold banding around cake and drum.

DECORATIONS

PL 837	Father Christmas on Skis
PL 1264	Happy Christmas Motto
H 2217	Gold & Green Holly with Roses
PL 765	Chalet
HP 1531	Holly Sprays (2)
BND 62	Gold Banding
BND 64	Gold Banding
	Round Drum

ICING TUBE

V 5083	Rope Tube No 14

MERRY CHRISTMAS

A very quick and simple cake to produce, it is full of bounce and Christmas cheer.

1 Rough-ice the top surface of the cake in Royal Icing.
2 Place a foil band around the side.
3 Pipe shells around the top edge using No 44 Tube.
4 Complete by placing holly around the edge and the plaque in the centre.

DECORATIONS

V 5225	Father Christmas Skating
ST 2462	Christmas Plaque
HP 1532	Holly Leaves
BND 78	Red Banding

ICING TUBE

V 5127	Rope Tube No 44

☆ Use a frill or banding to save decorating the sides.

RUDOLF THE REINDEER

Children will delight in being able to eat all the decorations on this attractive cake.

1 Having coated the top and sides of the cake with white Royal Icing, pipe shells around the top and bottom edges using No 18 Tube.
2 Place dragees in between each shell and allow to dry.
3 Complete by placing a frill around the side and the holly motto and plaque on top.

DECORATIONS

HP 1533	Holly Leaves (6)
SUG 947	Reindeer Plaque
SUG 946	Merry Christmas Motto
FR 1054	Frill
ST 2170	Dragees

ICING TUBE

V 5085	Rope Tube No 18

Cake decorators all seem to love a christening, which meant that we had a large and varied collection from which to make our choice On the whole the cakes shown are non-traditional, and there are one or two remarkable innovations.

WELCOME

A simply decorated cake with delicate pink ribbon and floral trim.

1 Cover the cake in Sugar Paste and allow to dry. Place on drum.
2 Pipe shells around the base of the cake using No 44 Tube.
3 Mark the lower side of the cake in scallops.
4 Gather 1in (2.5cm) wide pink ribbon and with Royal Icing attach to the sides of the cake, following the scallop markings.

5 Pipe over the top edge of the ribbon with shells.
6 Roll out Sugar Paste to approx. ¼in (6mm) thick, pattern the top surface and cut to an oval shape.
7 Place on the cake, pipe dots around the edge and allow to dry.
8 Add flower sprays to side and top of cake, and complete with the cradle.

DECORATIONS

S 6112PI	Pink Blossom
SN 117	Cradle with Pink Ribbon
BV 5027	Pink Satin Ribbon
F 5395PI	Pink Rosebuds
	Round Drum

ICING TUBES

V 5074	Plain Tube No 2
V 5127	Rope Tube No 44

SUGAR AND SPICE

The rhyme says: 'Sugar and spice and all things nice, That's what little girls are made of.' So here is a special cake for a very special girl.

1 Cover the cake in Sugar Paste and place on drum.
2 Pipe shells around the bottom edge using No 27 Tube.
3 Pipe 2 rows of dots around the sides approx. ½in (1.2cm) from the top edge and 1in (2.5cm) from the bottom edge.
4 With a No 1 Tube join together the dots with loops.
5 Pipe the name on top of the cake.
6 Place silver banding around the side of the cake.
7 Place a Christening ornament on top of the cake and complete by adding butterflies.

DECORATIONS

SN 117	Cradle with Pink Ribbon
BV 5149	Butterflies (22)
BND 63	Silver Banding
	Round Drum

ICING TUBE

V 5080	Star Tube No 27
V 5125	Plain Tube No 1

SPECIAL DELIVERY

The stork carrying the baby has long been symbolic of christening.

1 Make a sponge, layer and cover with Butter Cream. Place on drum.
2 Using a comb scraper, draw around the sides.
3 Mark the top of the cake into approx. 2in (5cm) segments and with No 1 Tube and brown coloured Butter Cream or chocolate, pipe the fine design illustrated.
4 Using white Butter Cream and No 2 Tube, pipe in each section as shown and add a dragee at each end.
5 Pipe shells around the top and bottom edges with the Star Tube.
6 Complete by adding silver storks, motto and stork ornament.

DECORATIONS

PL 1391	It's-A-Boy Motto
ST 2170	Dragees
SN 1BL	Stork with Flower & Bow
CP 1035	Silver Storks (4)
	Round Drum

ICING TUBES

V 5125	Plain Tube No 1
V 5074	Plain Tube No 2
TV 4869	Star Tube Size 5 .

PERFECTION

A Danish christening cake of pure artistry.

1 Make 1 large round and 1 small round cake, layer each in the usual way and cover in Butter Cream.
2 Cover each cake with a thin layer of marzipan and place the small tier on top of the large tier.
3 Attach gum paste leaves around the sides of the cake, also flower sprays and horseshoes as illustrated, using Royal Icing to fix.
4 Complete by placing cradle in position.

DECORATIONS

S 6112PI	Pink Blossom (12 here, but quantities vary with size of cake)
WVS 4527	Silver horseshoes (18)
C 18	Sugar Paste Leaves (20)
SN 117	Cradle with Pink Ribbon
	Round Drum

LULLABY

Here is something really special: a 'twins cake' from Australia.

1 Cover the cake in Plastic Icing and place on drum. Mark top in 2 ovals.
2 Roll out 2 strips of Plastic Icing 1in (2.5cm) wide to go round ovals. Wet edge and attach, impressing pattern with a fork. Flute edges.
3 Roll out another strip to go round bottom of cake. Attach and scallop edge.
4 Place ribbons around the side of cake.
5 Using Royal Icing and No 2 Tube, pipe dots on side and names on top.
6 Overpipe names with No 1 Tube. Tint oval edges in pink and blue using a fine paint brush.
7 Place on sprigs of heather, storks and Baby ornament.

DECORATIONS

SN 121	Baby on Plaque, Blue
SN 120	Baby on Plaque, Pink
CP 1035	Silver Storks (6)
WV 4484	Heather, 4 Pink, 4 Blue
BV 5027	Satin Ribbon
	Round Drum

ICING TUBES

V 5125	Plain Tube No 1
V 5074	Plain Tube No 2

CANADIAN CREAM

This novel and delicious cake came from Canada, where baby shower parties are ever-popular.

1 Make a sponge and cut to shape.
2 Cover cake in fresh whipped cream. Place on drum.
3 Using a Savoy Bag and Star Tube, pipe a rope design around the top edges of the body and handle.
4 Using the same tube, pipe vertical zigzag lines around sides of the wheels and a circular pattern around tops of wheels.
5 Cut Kiwi fruit into slices and place one slice on each wheel and half slices around pram body.
6 Place fresh strawberries between the Kiwi fruit. Pipe a small swirl of cream on each half slice of Kiwi fruit, and top with a melon ball.
7 Complete by adding melon balls and strawberries to handle of pram and motto in middle.

DECORATIONS

PL 1391	It's-A-Boy Motto
	Round Drum
	Assorted Fresh Fruit

ICING TUBES

TV 4873	Star Tube Size 9
TV 4949	Savoy Bag

The designs in this section are for those occasions when champagne and good food are served. Many of the cakes can easily be adapted to suit other special occasions, large or small.

MAGIC MOMENT

A very simple but attractive heart shaped engagement cake.

1 Cover cake in Sugar Paste and place on drum.
2 Pipe shells around the base of the cake with No 27 Tube.
3 Pipe dots on sides with No 2 Tube.
4 Using a small amount of Royal Icing, fix the doves on the sides of the cake.
5 Complete by adding the wishing well, flowers and motto.

DECORATIONS

V 5187	Wishing Well
S 6118	Ring of Flowers
CP 1088	Silver Doves (4)
CP 1070	Engagement Motto
	Heart Drum

ICING TUBES

V 5074	Plain Tube No 2
V 5080	Star Tube No 27

CONGRATULATIONS

1 Make and marzipan cake, place on drum and Royal-ice.
2 Pipe shells round base with No 44 Tube, and garlands round top edges.
3 Overpipe garlands with S scrolls using a No 43 Tube.
4 Following outline of garlands, pipe 3 parallel lines: outer line piped with No 3 Tube, middle line with No 2, inside line with No 1. Overpipe outside line with Nos 2 and 1 Tubes and middle line with No 1.
5 Overpipe S scrolls on the garlands in red with No 1 Tube and also pipe red dots between each shell.
6 Write inscription, overpipe in red and add decorations.

DECORATIONS

WVS 4540	Silver Horseshoe
S 6109RE	Roses & Leaves (4)
WE 20RE	Wafer Roses (3)
L 301	Silver Leaves (2)
BV 5027RE	Red Satin Ribbon
BND 63	Silver Banding

ICING TUBES

V 5125	Plain Tube No 1
V 5074	Plain Tube No 2
V 5075	Plain Tube No 3
V 5126	Rope Tube No 43
V 5127	Rope Tube No 44

ROMANCE

This evocative open book cake can be used to celebrate all kinds of occasions, including weddings, engagements, anniversaries and landmarks in family life.

1 Bake an oblong cake, and cut the 'fore-edge' sides of the book to slope gently.
2 The 'book' shape can be more easily moulded when covering the top with marzipan; cover the sides as well.
3 Place cake on drum and cover with Royal Icing, leaving the top surface smooth and drawing a comb scraper horizontally around the sides to give a page effect.
4 Ice the drum and allow to dry.
5 Roll out pink coloured Sugar Paste and cut out 1in (2.5cm) wide strips; place around base of cake.
6 Pipe a shell edge around the top of the book and the edge of the drum with No 43 Tube, and add the inscription on the book.
7 Complete by adding the silver bands and decorations as illustrated.

DECORATIONS

S 55	White Flowers & Silver Leaves (2)
S 6110PI	Treble Pink Roses & Leaves with Bow (3)
CP 1056	Silver Congratulations Motto
S 3082	Horseshoes & Blossom (4)
BND 63	Silver Banding
BND 67	Silver Banding
	Square Drum

ICING TUBES

V 5125	Plain Tube No 1
V 5126	Rope Tube No 43

MELODY

This beautiful novelty cake would grace any grand occasion.

1 Bake a square cake. Make a template of a grand piano and cut cake to this shape.
2 Using the same template, cut out two cake cards.
3 Cut a step out of the cake for the keyboard, Cover the cake with marzipan and then with Sugar Paste.
4 Place the cake on one of the shaped cards, and before the paste has dried mark the sides of the piano with marzipan tweezers.
5 Cover the second shaped card in Sugar Paste and decorate with marzipan tweezers as for the side of the piano.
6 Pipe shells around the lid and bottom edge of the piano with No 43 Tube.
7 Using No 1 Tube, pipe strings on top of the piano.
8 Place a thin strip of silver banding around the piano.
9 With No 1 Tube and black coloured icing, pipe the piano keys.
10 Place blossom around the side of the cake.
11 Place on lid, using a cocktail stick to keep it open.
12 Complete by adding motto to lid and place cake on pillars.

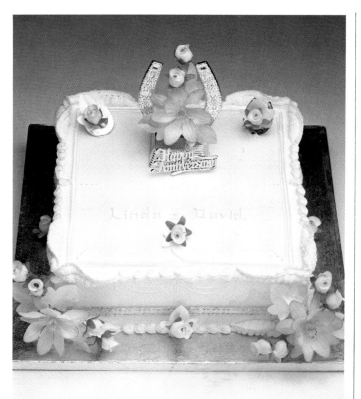

SPECIAL OCCASION

A luxurious cake for an important
gathering.

1 Cover cake in Royal Icing.
2 Pipe S scrolls on corners and shells
between each scroll, using No 44 Tube.
3 Overpipe scrolls twice with Nos 3
and 2 Tubes and then with small
lilac coloured dots using No 1 Tube.
4 Pipe 3 straight parallel lines on
each side of the top of the cake,
using Nos 3, 2 and 1 Tubes;
overpipe No 3 with No 2, and Nos 1
and 2 with No 1.
5 With No 1 Tube, pipe on names.
6 Complete by adding decorations.

DECORATIONS

S 6129	Lilac Sprays (4)
SN 115	Horseshoe
S 6108WH	Single White Rose
WVS 4540	Silver Horseshoes (2)
F 5395 WH	White Rosebuds (7)
	Square Drum

ICING TUBES

V 5125	Plain Tube No 1
V 5074	Plain Tube No 2
V 5075	Plain Tube No 3
V 5126	Rope Tube No 43
V 5127	Rope Tube No 44

DECORATIONS

F 5396	Blue Blossom (6)
PP 6233	Square Silver Pillars (3)
L 301	Leaves (6)
CP 1056	Silver Congratulations Motto
S 3089	White Blossom (2)
BND 65	Silver Banding
	Thin Silver Boards (2)

ICING TUBES

V 5125	Plain Tube No 1
V 5126	Rope Tube No 43

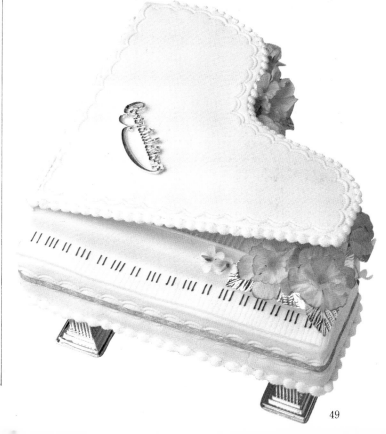

TOGETHERNESS

A traditional gold wedding cake enhanced by the interesting use of gold banding and a beautiful spray of flowers.

1 Having Royal-iced the cake in the usual way until flat and smooth, fix pieces of 1in (2.5cm) gold banding diagonally across the top corners and vertically at the angles.
2 Pipe S scrolls with Rope Tube No 44 on each corner, as illustrated.
3 Pipe dots in the middle of each scroll.
4 Using No 4 Tube, overpipe the scrolls.
5 Complete by adding decorations to the sides and top of cake.

DECORATIONS

S 6109YE	Yellow Double Roses & Leaves with Bow (3)
S 52	White Flowers (2)
F 5403	White Blossom (8)
WVG 4527	Gold Horseshoes (4)
WV 4484WH	White Heather (4)
BND 64	Gold Banding
	Square Gold Drum

ICING TUBES

V 5076	Plain Tube No 4
V 5127	Rope Tube No 44

ELEGANCE

The delicate decorations serve to make this a wedding anniversary cake of model elegance.

1 Make the cake in an oval tin. Marzipan and cover with Plastic Icing.
2 Place on drum and with a Star Tube pipe shells around the bottom edge.
3 When dry, fasten ribbon around the sides.
4 Using No 2 Tube, pipe the pattern on the side as illustrated.
5 Complete by adding the decorations.

DECORATIONS

PL 1395	25th Silver Numerals
S 6105	White Flowers (6)
F 5395PI	Pink Rosebuds (8)
CP 1088	Silver Doves (2)
WV 4609	Silver Slippers
V 5279WH	White Decorette Ribbon
	Round Drum

ICING TUBES

V 5074	Plain Tube No 2
V 5080	Star Tube No 27

☆ Oval cakes look well on a square drum.

PRECIOUS MOMENT

1 Cover cake in Royal Icing until flat and smooth. Place on drum.
2 Pipe shells around base with No 18 Tube and S scrolls around top.
3 Overpipe the top and bottom borders three times using Nos 3, 2 and 1 Tubes.
4 Place on ornament, and with No 1 Tube pipe latticework between the ornament and the cake, initials on either side of the ornament, and names on the side.
5 Also on the side of the cake pipe a pale green stem using No 1 Tube, and green leaves with No 66 Tube.
6 Add horseshoe, flowers and ornament to complete.

DECORATIONS

CP 1072	Silver Horseshoes (4)
S 6107	Flowers & Leaves (7)
SN 107	Happy Anniversary Ornament
	Round Drum

ICING TUBES

V 5125	Plain Tube No 1
V 5074	Plain Tube No 2
V 5075	Plain Tube No 3
V 5085	Rope Tube No 18
V 5092	Leaf Tube No 66

GOLDEN DAYS

Fresh cream and rich gold are combined in this Canadian creation to present a cake that all the guests will find irresistible.

1 Place the base cake on drum, layer with cream, tier cakes and cover in whipped cream.
2 Place gold banding around each tier.
3 Using Star Tube Size 7, pipe a rope pattern around the bottom edge of the cake and around the top edge of each tier.
4 Place on gold decorations and complete with the top ornament.

DECORATIONS

SN 112	Gold Horseshoe Ornament
ST 2460	Bells (8)
WVG 4527	Gold Horseshoes (8)
BND 66	Gold Banding
BND 62	Gold Banding
	Round Drum

ICING TUBE

TV 4871	Star Tube Size 7

In this section we have
something for High Days, Happy
Days and Holidays. When
making our selection we looked
for both novelty and flexibility.
Now you can give full rein to your
skill and imagination.

LADIES DAY

Here is something a little more
ambitious – a straw boater cake
with basket weave, ideal for sunny
days or any festive occasion.

1 Place cake on drum and cover in a
thin coat of Royal Icing or Sugar
Paste.
2 Pipe the cake and top of the drum
in basket weave, using white Royal
Icing for the basket tube and green
Royal Icing for the plain tube.
3 When dry, place ribbon around
the side of the cake, make a bow
and attach to the side.
4 Complete by fixing flowers around
the brim and on top of the hat.

DECORATIONS

F 5396BL	Blue Polyester Flowers (5)
F 5396WH	White Cloth Flowers (4)
S 6110BL	Treble Blue Roses & Leaves with Bow (2)
WV 4484WH	White Heather (2)
WV 4484BL	Blue Heather (2)
L 301	Silver Rose Leaves (6)
BV 5027BL	Blue Satin Ribbon
	Round Drum

ICING TUBES

V 5078	Plain Tube No 6
V 5094	Basket Tube No 47

EASTER BONNET

Hats are back in fashion!

1 Place the cake on card approx. 4in
(10cm) larger in diameter than the
cake, and cover the cake and top of
the card in white Sugar Paste.
2 When dry, place 2 ribbons around
the side of the cake.
3 Using No 3 Tube and Royal Icing,
pipe dots along the edges of the
ribbons and the edge of the card.
4 Make a ribbon bow and attach to
the cake.
5 Place on wafer roses and Happy
Easter motto.

DECORATIONS

WE 20	Assorted small Wafer Roses (18)
BV 5027WH	White Satin Ribbon
PL 1310	Happy Easter Motto
	Cake Card

ICING TUBE

V 5075	Plain Tube No 3

EASTER CASKET

A lovely surprise for Easter!

1 Using a Swiss roll for the basic
cake, cover in either pink Sugar
Paste which has a basket weave
pattern impressed on it, or cover
with marzipan and, using Royal
Icing, pipe basket weave in the
usual way.
2 With No 44 Tube pipe shells
around the top edge, and overpipe
shells with a loop movement using
No 2 Tube.
3 Place banding around bottom and
ribbon around side, tying in a bow.
4 Complete with chenille rabbit.

DECORATIONS

V 4941	Chenille Rabbit
V 5279	Pink Ribbon
BND 62	Gold Banding

ICING TUBES

V 5074	Plain Tube No 2
V 5127	Rope Tube No 44

SUGAR EASTER EGGS

The decorating of sweets and candy grows ever more popular. These eggs show just two of the dozens of ways to create a memorable effect.

1 Press Sugar Paste firmly into chocolate or sugar egg moulds, cut off excess paste and leave to dry.
2 When dry, turn out of mould.
3 With Royal Icing and No 1 Tube, pipe either a latticework design, as illustrated on the small half-egg, or that featured on the green half-egg.
4 Pipe shells around the base of the half-eggs using a No 44 Tube and complete by adding the decorations.

DECORATIONS (White Egg)

WV 4484BL	Blue Heather
L 1912	Silver Leaves (2)
BV 5149	Butterfly

DECORATIONS (Green Egg)

BV 5149	Butterfly
ST 2170	Silver Dragees
BND 62	Gold Banding

ICING TUBES

V 5125	Plain Tube No 1
V 5127	Rope Tube No 44

MOTHERING SUNDAY

A bunch of violets for Mother has long been a Mother's Day tradition. This cake is the present that all the family can enjoy.

1 Cover the cake and top of the drum in white Royal Icing.
2 Pipe shells around the top and bottom edges, using a Rope Tube.
3 Place violets on top of the cake and on the drum.
4 Using a No 2 Tube and white Royal Icing, pipe flower stems for the violets.
5 With green icing in the No 2 Tube, pipe leaves on the stems, and pipe a loop around the shells and the edge of the drum.
6 Place the Mother's Day motto on the cake and complete by edging the drum in 1in (2.5cm) gold banding and placing ribbons and bows around the side of the cake.

DECORATIONS

PL 1407	Mother's Day Motto
SF 121	Sugar Violets (17)
SF 7	Sugar Flowers (2)
BND 64	Gold Banding
	Yellow Ribbon

ICING TUBES

V 5074	Plain Tube No 2
V 5127	Rope Tube No 44

SURPRISE

This versatile celebration cake can be filled with all kinds of sweets, fruits or small presents.

1 Place the marzipanned cake off-centre on a drum at least 3in (8cm) larger in diameter than the cake, and coat in Royal Icing.
2 Take a thin card the same diameter as the cake, coat in Royal Icing and allow to dry.
3 Mark lid into 1in (2.5cm) squares, and overpipe markings with small shells using No 16 Tube.
4 Pipe shells on top of cake with No 18 Tube, also on top and bottom edges and around edge of lid.
5 Stick sugar flowers on lid and 1in (2.5cm) silver banding around cake, and place lid in position.
6 Fill the centre of the cake with marzipan fruits, etc.

DECORATIONS

ST 2174	Sugar Flowers
ST 2175	Marzipan Fruits
BND 65	Silver Banding
	Cake Card
	Round Drum

ICING TUBES

V 5084	Rope Tube No 16
V 5085	Rope Tube No 18

SPRINGTIME

An eye-catching cake full of flowers and an Easter basket.

1 Make cake then: *either* cover in Sugar Paste and emboss a basket pattern, *or* pipe a basket weave design in Royal Icing.
2 To make basket lid, take a card the same diameter as cake, cut in half and cover with basket pattern.
3 Place cake on drum, ice drum and pipe shells with No 43 Tube.
4 Place flowers on cake, joining them together with Royal Icing.
5 Using the Leaf Tube, pipe leaves between flowers and add lid.
6 Using No 2 Tube, pipe linework around the top edge of the drum and add all other decorations.

DECORATIONS

PL 1310	Happy Easter Motto
V 4936	Small Chicks (2)
BV 5149	Butterflies (2)
SF 22	Sugar Roses (6)

SF 7	Sugar Flowers (12)
	Green Ribbon
	Round Cake Card
	Round Drum

ICING TUBES

V 5074	Plain Tube No 2
V 5075	Plain Tube No 3 (if basket weave piped)
V 5094	Basket Tube No 47 (if basket weave piped)
V 5126	Rope Tube No 43
V 5093	Leaf Tube No 68

MOTHER'S CRINOLINE CAKE

Another occasion and another version of this striking and popular cake.

1 Having made the cake in the correct shape, cover in marzipan and place off-centre on the drum.
2 Roll out green coloured Sugar Paste, pattern the surface and place on front of Crinoline Lady.
3 Roll out pink coloured Sugar Paste approx. 12in (30cm) in diameter, place over drum and cake, cut out a section to allow the green panel to show, neatly fold back the edge and pleat the paste on the drum to give a gown effect.
4 Roll out additional pink Sugar Paste for the train, texture the surface and place on cake.
5 Fix the Crinoline Lady on top, and complete by adding dragees, blossom and motto.

DECORATIONS

ST 2117	Dragees
PX 1150	Crinoline Lady
WV 5015	Blossom (10)
PL 1407	Mother's Day Motto

SWEETHEART

A gingerbread heart for Valentine's Day.

1 Having made the gingerbread heart, place it on a heart shaped drum.
2 With No 2 Tube and white Royal Icing, pipe hearts on top of the gingerbread as illustrated.
3 Soften the Royal Icing until it flows, divide into four different coloured icings and fill in the heart as shown.
4 Allow to dry; to speed up setting and to give a high-gloss finish, place the cake under a reading light.
5 Using No 1 Tube and white Royal Icing, pipe trelliswork over the pink heart.
6 Pipe stars around the side of the gingerbread and on the edge of the drum.
7 Pipe rope edging around the pink heart, dots around the green heart and shells around the brown heart.
8 Place wafer roses, butterflies and heart on the cake, and fix red ribbon around the side of the drum.

DECORATIONS

WE 21RE	Red Wafer Roses (8)
BV 5027RE	Red Satin Ribbon
BV 5149	Butterflies (2)
CP 1074	Single Heart
L 326	Wafer Leaves (8)
	Heart Drum

ICING TUBES

V 5125	Plain Tube No 1
V 5074	Plain Tube No 2
V 5083	Rope Tube No 14
V 5086	Rope Tube No 20

Before starting your cake, make sure that you have all the correct ingredients, equipment and decorations.

☆ If gingerbread is not your favourite, try a sponge or madeira base.

AULD LANG SYNE

The words have meaning wherever New Year is celebrated. This cake was designed in Singapore, and there red means good luck.

1 Coat cake in Butter Cream and divide the top into 8 sections.
2 Using a Star Tube, pipe garlands around the top between each section.
3 With the same tube outline the garlands with a curved line, using either chocolate or chocolate Butter Cream, and then with a No 2 Tube continue to outline the garlands 3 more times, as illustrated.
4 With the No 2 Tube, pipe the inscription and flower stems.
5 Pipe leaves in green Royal Icing using a Leaf Tube.
6 Add wafer roses on top and complete by placing a frill around the side of the cake.

DECORATIONS

FR 609	Cake Frill
WE 21RE	Red Wafer Roses (4)
WE 20PI	Pink Wafer Roses (8)
	Round Drum

ICING TUBES

V 5074	Plain Tube No 2
TV 4869	Star Tube Size 5
V 5093	Leaf Tube No 68

BULLSEYE

1 Cover the cake in marzipan and place on drum.
2 Cover the sides and top of drum in red Sugar Paste.
3 Divide the top into 20 equal segments.
4 Make a template of one segment.
5 Roll out yellow Sugar Paste and cut out 10 segments; leave to partly set.
6 Roll out black Sugar Paste and cut out 10 more segments; leave to partly set.
7 Place alternately coloured segments around top of cake, then with a pastry cutter cut out the middle section. Roll out red Sugar Paste and use the cutter to cut out a circle; position this in the centre of the cake.
8 Place numerals, Happy Birthday motto and dart on the cake.

DECORATIONS

PL 1292 – 1301	Plastic Numerals
PL 1315	Happy Birthday Motto
	Round Drum

☆ Black colouring is only available at certain retail outlets, but another contrasting colour can be just as effective.

57

DOMINO

A novel cake for any gathering.

1 Using a Battenberg type of cake, roll out brown coloured Sugar Paste and cut out sides of domino box.
2 Mark the sides with a stiff brush to give a wood grain effect.
3 Roll out black coloured Sugar Paste and cover the top surface.
4 Mark the top surface with domino shapes using a palette knife.
5 The dots are made by pressing No 1 Tube into the surface of the paste and filling the indentations with soft white Royal Icing.
6 Fix the sides in position and place cake on drum.
7 Using alphabet letters make up the word 'Retirement' and fasten to the side of the cake. Complete by adding Best Wishes motto on top, and banding around drum.

DECORATIONS

CP 1066	Best Wishes Motto
PL 1399	Plastic Letters & Numbers Set
BND 63	Silver Banding

ICING TUBE

V 5125	Plain Tube No 1

CHEERS

Here is a great idea for a special birthday or celebration.

1 Make a sheet of Genoese cake approx. 10in (25cm) square by 2in (5cm) deep, and using a large pastry cutter approx. 4in (10cm) in diameter cut out circles.
2 Layer together until cake is approx. 8in (20cm) high.
3 Cover the sides in brown coloured Sugar Paste and press in the back of a knife handle to give a dimple effect.
4 Roll out white Sugar Paste to the diameter of the beer mug and place on top of cake.
5 With dusted fingers gently shape the top of the paste to give a foam effect.
6 Roll out more white Sugar Paste in a sausage shape approx. 6in (15cm) long, shape into the handle of the mug and leave to set.
7 When set, fix the handle to the side of the mug, place mug on drum and add decorations as illustrated.

DECORATIONS

CP 1084	Congratulations Motto
ST 2505	Number 1
ST 2512	Number 8

TECHNIQUES OF CAKE DECORATING

Now you have seen the tempting array of cake decorating ideas set out in the previous section, you will probably be raring to try one of those designs.

If you are an experienced cake decorator you will know most of, if not all, the methods used for decorating the cakes illustrated.

Let us suppose that you are a student or have never decorated a cake before. In this section we have included easy step by step instructions on the techniques and methods required to produce all the cakes in the book.

When learning to decorate, use the basic techniques first and gradually increase your skill. With decorating, practice *does* make perfect, so the more time you can spend practising, the better the results you can look forward to.

Finally, skill also needs to be developed to apply the cake decorations, to ensure that the cake is correctly balanced and that the decorations further enhance your masterpiece.

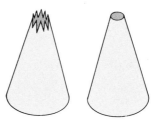

COVERING THE CAKE

With most types of icings it is necessary or advisable to cover the base cake with Marzipan or Almond Paste. This provides a good foundation for the icing and prevents the cake staining the icing.

Although cakes decorated with Butter Cream are not usually covered with Marzipan or Almond Paste a thin covering can ease the application of the Butter Cream and improve the eating quality of the cake.

Icing recipes are listed at the end of this section. Here we look at how to apply the various coverings to finished cakes.

MARZIPAN

1 Warm and work the Marzipan until it is pliable. Sprinkle icing sugar or caster sugar on the board or table to prevent sticking, and roll out to the desired size and thickness.

2 Cut out enough to cover the top of the cake.

3 Roll out the remaining Marzipan into an oblong shape and, when this is long enough to go round the cake, cut the sides straight and level and gently roll up the strip like a Swiss roll.

4 Lightly cover the cake with boiled Apricot Jam (see Recipes). This seals the cake and ensures the Marzipan or Almond Paste stays firmly attached.

5 Place on the top covering of Marzipan/Almond Paste and, using a rolling pin, roll until flat, smooth and level.

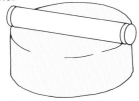

6 Turn cake upside down and place Marzipan/Almond Paste around side. Using a straight-sided utensil, roll Marzipan around side until it is upright and smooth.

7 Allow a few days for the Marzipan to dry before icing. This prevents the oils in the Marzipan from penetrating and discolouring the icing.

8 When marzipanning cakes for the Australian style of decorating, a slightly different method is required. Instead of using 2 pieces of Marzipan, roll out 1 piece large enough to cover top and sides. Apply in the usual way but ensuring that a smooth curve is produced between the top and sides of the cake.

> **Be careful not to over-knead marzipan as this will break down the oil content and stain your icing.**

SUGAR PASTE

1 For best results, make sure that your cake has a good flat surface, since Sugar Paste tends to highlight any uneven areas. An initial coat of Marzipan will usually provide the right working base.

2 Using cornflour as a dusting agent, roll out the Sugar Paste and apply as for Marzipan (see above).

3 Finish off by smoothing any unevenness with your fingers. These should be well dusted in cornflour.

4 If you want to give your Sugar Paste a patterned surface, there are various ways of introducing a pattern, as follows:

    a Press the back of a straight knife into the paste to form grooves.
    b By changing the direction of the knife you can impress diamond and square patterns in the paste.
    c Patterned rollers or utensils with patterned surfaces can also be used, rotating them against the cake until the desired effect is achieved.

5 To join two pieces of Sugar Paste together, moisten both surfaces with water and gently press together; smooth the join by rubbing gently with a floured finger.

ROYAL ICING

1 Position the cake on a drum and fix with Royal Icing.

2 Using a palette knife, spread the icing over the top and sides of the cake with a forward and backward motion to ensure even distribution and to disperse any large bubbles in the icing.

3 A smooth surface can be produced by using either the palette knife or a straight-edged ruler on the top.

    a Place palette knife on top of cake and rotate until top is smooth.
    b With a straight-edged ruler draw forward and back across the cake until the surface is level and smooth.

4 To smooth the sides, hold the palette knife upright and draw around or across the sides until they are level and smooth. Alternatively, a straight-edged plastic scraper can be used and a similar method employed. Remove any surplus icing from the drum and top edges.

5 If the top edges of the cake are to be piped, it is helpful if they are bevelled by holding the palette knife at an angle of approx. 40 degrees to the cake and drawing gently around the edges, removing surplus icing to leave a slight angle on the edge.

6 When coating a cake with Royal Icing, we recommend that at least 3 coats be applied; the first and last should be thin. Leave the cake to dry between each coat and remove any lumps or rough icing with a knife before commencing the next coat.

> **Sugar Paste is very delicate and must be handled carefully. It is especially useful for decorating difficult shapes.**

BUTTER CREAM
For Butter Cream the same method of covering is used as for Royal Icing, but only 1 coat is applied.

DECORATIVE ICING
ICING BAG
Before you can begin piping you will need one essential piece of equipment – an icing bag. This can easily be made at home, using greaseproof paper and scissors.

1 Cut a piece of greaseproof paper in the form of a right-angled triangle (half a perfect square).

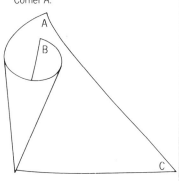

2 Take Corner B and fold it round into Corner A.

> **Stir Royal Icing well before use to remove air bubbles.**

3 Bring Corner C round the outside so that it lies directly behind A.

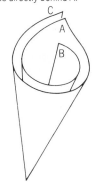

4 Push all the corners of the bag neatly together and make sure that the point of the bag (D) is quite closed.

5 Fold over several times at the A–B–C join to keep the bag together. Snip a small piece off the point at D.

6 The bag is now ready. Insert icing tube and fill bag with icing. Be careful not to over-fill. Fold top of bag to prevent icing from spilling out.

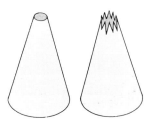

PIPING – THE FIRST STAGES
Begin by practising straight and wavy lines on the back of a plate or on a practice board. Use a small Plain Tube, hold the bag and push out the icing through thumb pressure. When you have almost reached the end of a line of icing, release the thumb pressure and lay down the end of the line, touching the board with the point of the tube to break it off. Once you are proficient at piping continuous smooth lines, you are ready to move on to pattern work.

Trellis Icing
The basic trellis consists of a series of straight parallel lines with a matching series piped over the top at right-angles. Variations on this idea include piping the upper series of lines in a diagonal direction, at 45 degrees to the lower series, and the interwoven trellis shown in the diagram.

Before you begin any kind of trellis icing, make sure that there are no large air bubbles in the icing since these would cause continual breaks in the fine lines and spoil the overall effect.

To make the interwoven trellis, proceed as follows:

1 Mark the outline shape of the area you intend to cover with trellis.

2 Working from the 10 o'clock position on your outline, pipe a straight line diagonally to the 4 o'clock position, using a round Plain Tube. Then pipe a second line over the top and at right-angles, i.e. from 1 o'clock to 7 o'clock.

3 Once these 2 guidelines are in position, complete your trellis pattern with alternate diagonal lines, with each parallel line approx. $\frac{1}{8}$in (3mm) from the one before.

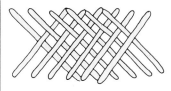

4 Using a sharp knife, gently remove any strands of piping that have overlapped the pattern area, and finish by piping around the outline.

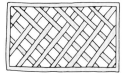

Lacework

This is a simple yet most attractive type of decoration.

1 Prepare your outline as for trellis work.

2 Using the same round tube, pipe continuous wiggly lines until the whole area is covered; the lines should not conform to any geometric pattern.

3 Finish as for trellis work.

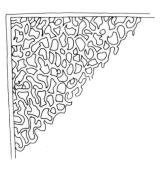

Basket Weave

This looks extremely complicated, but is in fact relatively simple to carry out, provided due care is taken to be neat and tidy the whole way round the cake.

1 With a sharp knife, mark the sides of the cake into equal vertical sections 1in (2.5cm) wide.

2 Using a Plain Tube No 2, pipe 2 adjacent vertical lines 1in (2.5cm) apart (a and b on diagram).

3 Using a Basket Tube, pipe the first 3 horizontal sections marked in the diagram, working in numerical order. Once this first section is complete, pipe in the next 2 vertical lines (c and d) and the next 3 horizontal sections (4, 5 and 6).

4 Follow this pattern round the entire cake, then apply to the top of the cake, working across from left to right.

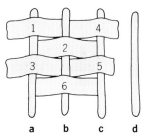

Always use good quality ingredients and equipment.

Dots

These are a very useful decoration, both easy to do and versatile in that they can be piped in simple rows, or joined with patterns of lines and loops. To make, hold the bag upright and pipe until a dot of the required size has formed. Pull the tube away quickly to break off.

It is important to have icing of the correct consistency for making well shaped dots. It should be slightly softer than for other piping work.

Shells

Using a Star Tube in the icing bag, hold the bag at an angle of 80 degrees. Press the bag until icing touches the cake, forming a bulb of the required size. Gently reduce the pressure and draw the tube away, ending the shell with a point.

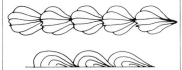

Swirls

Using a large Star Tube, hold the bag upright. Pipe icing on to the cake until the correct diameter of swirl is obtained. Then, raising the tube slowly and turning it in a circular motion, gradually reduce the pressure to give a final tapering effect.

C and S Scrolls

These are a variation of the shell, with an extra 'tail'. Pipe them as for shells, but make them at least twice as long and smoothly curved in the shape of a C or S.

COMB SCRAPERS AND RULERS

Several cakes illustrated in this book have been decorated with the aid of a comb scraper. A scraper is a thin piece of plastic with either a straight or serrated edge. You can buy one ready-made or create your own by taking a plastic set square and carefully cutting V shaped grooves along one side with a sharp knife. Use the scraper to spread the icing on the cake instead of a palette knife, holding it firmly between thumb and fingers and drawing it round or over the cake until the pattern is completed.

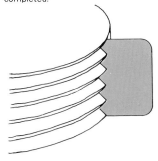

The most common types of pattern are straight and undulating. To achieve the latter, simply add a slight up and down motion as you draw the scraper round.

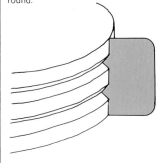

TEMPLATES

Before you begin to make a celebration cake, it is a good idea to make a rough sketch of it, drawing in any detailed work which you plan to pipe on the cake. This will help to ensure that the cake has an attractive design and is well balanced. To transfer your decorative designs to the cake, you will probably need to make a template. These are easy to turn out, using either thin card or paper. Below are simple instructions for making templates for the tops and sides of both round and square cakes.

Round Cake

Top Cut out a piece of paper or card to the same diameter as the cake.

Fold it in half, then in half again, continuing until it has the same number of segments as the design. Pencil the shape you wish to repeat on the paper, then cut out with scissors.

Sides Cut your paper or card to match the whole of the side of the cake. Fold it in half, then in half again, continuing until it has the same number of segments as the design. Pencil the shape you wish to repeat on the paper, then cut out with scissors.

Square Cake

Top Cut your paper or card to make a square the same size as the cake. Fold it in half, then in half again, and finally fold diagonally. As with the round cake, pencil your shape and cut out.

Sides The method is the same as for the round cake, except that your template should be as long as just one side of the square. When it is cut out, you can use this template for each side.

Using the Template

Whatever its shape, use your template by placing it against the surface of the cake and scoring the design on it with the tip of a sharp knife or similar object. This leaves you a clear and accurate pattern to follow when you begin piping.

> **When making a heavy fruit cake, bake at least 3 months in advance to allow the cake to mature.**

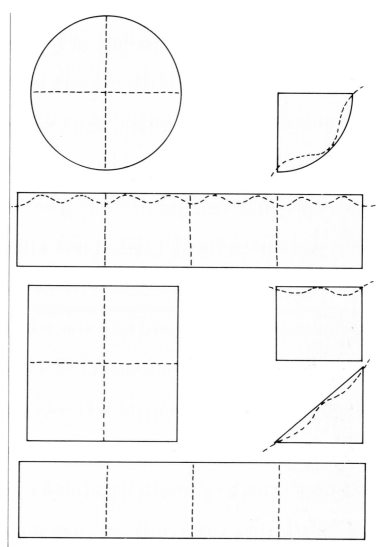

ICING RECIPES

BUTTER CREAM
Sufficient for 1 x 10in (25.4cm) cake

8oz (225g) unsalted butter or margarine
1lb (450g) icing sugar
flavouring and colouring as required

Mix the ingredients together and beat well. Butter or margarine should be at room temperature; warm slightly if cold. The more you beat, the better the results. Add flavouring and colouring as required.

> **It may be necessary to alter the amount of liquid in recipes. This is because the water absorption may vary in the dry ingredients.**

SUGAR PASTE
Sufficient for 1 x 8in (20cm) round cake

1lb (450g) icing sugar
1 egg white
2oz (57g) liquid glucose
2–4 tsp lemon juice
plus, for a soft texture, 1 tsp glycerine

Sieve the icing sugar into a bowl, mix in the egg white and all the liquid ingredients (first warming the glucose to make mixing easier). Mix together, turn out on a lightly dusted board and knead to a firm smooth paste. Add extra icing sugar if necessary. Colouring: Add food colours to produce the right colour. Always begin slowly, building up the colour gradually until you achieve the shade you want. Knead thoroughly to make sure the colour is evenly distributed.

ROYAL ICING
Sufficient for 1 x 8 or 9in (20 or 22.8cm) cake

2lb (900g) icing sugar
4 egg whites (large)
1 tsp lemon juice
2 tsp glycerine (optional)
blue colouring (optional)

Sieve half the icing sugar into a bowl, add the egg whites and mix well. Add the rest of the icing sugar in small batches, stir in well before adding the next. Add the lemon juice, glycerine and beat together for 5-10 minutes until it is light. Leave to rest for at least 1 hour before use, covering with a damp cloth.

To improve the whiteness of the icing, add a small amount of blue colouring.

APRICOT JAM

1 lb (450g) apricot jam
1 tbsp water

Add water to jam and gently bring to the boil. Spread on cake with either a palette knife or pastry brush.

HOW MUCH DO YOU NEED?

Use the following as an approximate guide to how much Marzipan and Royal Icing are needed over a range of cake sizes. The quantities are approximate because the amounts needed will also depend on how thickly you intend to apply them.

PLASTIC ICING

Sufficient for 1 x 10in (25.4cm) cake

2 fl oz (57ml) water
1 tbsp gelatine
2 tsp glycerine
3 tbsp liquid glucose
1½lb (680g) icing sugar
approx. ½lb (225g) icing sugar for kneading

Place water in a saucepan, add gelatine and stir over a low heat until it is dissolved; do not allow to boil. Remove from heat, add glycerine and glucose and stir until completely blended; allow to cool. Place sieved icing sugar in a mixing bowl, add cooled mixture and blend together. When mixture becomes difficult to stir, turn out on to a sugared board and knead in remaining icing sugar until mixture is smooth and has lost its stickiness. Place in an air-tight container until required.

Always ensure that equipment is thoroughly clean.

SUPERIOR PLASTIC ICING

Sufficient for a small 3 tier or medium 2 tier cake

A
5fl oz (145ml) water
4oz (110g) liquid glucose
1lb (450g) granulated sugar
1fl oz (30ml) glycerine
1 tsp cream of tartar

B
5fl oz (145ml) water
1oz (30g) gelatine
4oz (110g) shortening
4½lb (2kg) icing sugar

Place all the 'A' ingredients in a saucepan and boil to 250°F (120°C), using a sugar boiling thermometer. Remove and allow to cool. Dissolve gelatine in second batch of water and add to cooled mixture. Cut shortening into small pieces and mix in. When mixture has cooled to lukewarm, gradually mix in half the sieved icing sugar. Place mixture in an air-tight container and leave for a few days. Before use, knead remainder of icing sugar into mixture until smooth.

Cake Size		Ingredients	
Square	Round	Marzipan (Almond Paste)	Royal Icing
—	6in (15cm)	1lb (450g)	1lb (450g)
6in (15cm)	7in (17.8cm)	1¼lb (560g)	1½lb (680g)
7in (17.8cm)	8in (20cm)	1½lb (680g)	1¾lb (790g)
8in (20cm)	9in (22.8cm)	2lb (900g)	2lb (900g)
9in (22.8cm)	10in (25.4cm)	2¼lb (1kg)	2¼lb (1kg)
10in (25.4cm)	11in (27.9cm)	2½lb (1.1kg)	2¾lb (1.2kg)
11in (27.9cm)	12in (30.4cm)	2¾lb (1.2kg)	3lb (1.4kg)
12in (30.4cm)	—	3lb (1.4kg)	3¼lb (1.5kg)

CATALOGUE

Here is the place to go window-shopping for all your cake decorations, in a wonderland of ornaments, animals, traditional figures like Father Christmas, novelties, flowers, mottoes and frills for every occasion.

Items are listed according to their position in the illustration, generally working from left to right and top to bottom. Where two different pattern numbers appear on the same line, this means that the item is available in two different types of packaging.

Sizes are listed for all wedding ornaments, since their dimensions vary considerably. In the other photographs, sizes are usually given of just one or two items which are generally representative of the others shown.

Wedding ornaments are packed in attractive, strong window display cartons. Where a second pattern number is shown, this indicates ornament available in bulk packs without display carton.

WEDDING ORNAMENTS

WON 112	Modest spray of lilies encircled by white flowers; 9 x 7in (22.8 x 17.8cm).
WON 721	Traditional archway of bridal bells, flowers, dove and ring; 9in (22.8cm).
WON 115	Delicate lace crown with pastel rosebuds nestling inside; 9 x 6in (22.8 x 15cm).

WEDDING ORNAMENTS

WON 781 The traditional wedding slipper filled with roses and feathers; 6in (15cm).

WON 119 Romantic pink rosebuds against a silver heart; 6in (15cm).

WON 792 Coronet of white flowers encircling a prayer book; 6in (15cm).

WON 113 Elevated white floral bouquet; 7 x 6in (17.8 x 15cm).

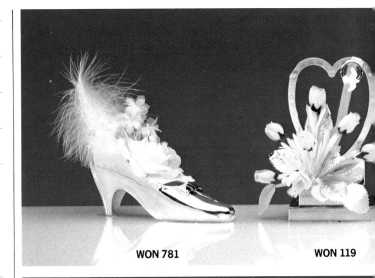

WON 781   WON 119

WON 105 Embossed silver horseshoe, arrayed with pink flowers and rosebuds; $5\frac{1}{2}$ x $3\frac{1}{2}$in (13.9 x 8.9cm).

WON 104 Peach floral spray, set in a silver horseshoe; $4\frac{1}{2}$ x $5\frac{1}{2}$in (11.4 x 13.3cm).

WON 787 White rose and flowers in large traditional horseshoe; $6\frac{3}{4}$in (17.1cm). Also WON 117.

WON 599 Roses and wedding bells in lucky silver horseshoe; 6in (15cm).

WON 105   WON 104

WON 110 A springtime fantasy of lilac coloured blossom in a silver basket; 9in (22.8cm).

WON 116 A basket of white lace and peach coloured blossom; 7in (17.8cm).

WON 716 A plumed rose cradled in a silver basket; 9in (22.8cm).

WON 111 A springtime fantasy of pink blossom in a silver basket; 9in (22.8cm).

WON 110   WON 116

WON 792   **WON 113**

WON 787   **WON 599**

WON 716   **WON 111**

WON 782 A wedded couple under a floral arch – with the added sophistication of a musical box; 7in (17.8cm).

WON 700 Bride and groom exchanging vows under a floral arch; 8in (20cm).

WON 793 Graceful couple beneath Edwardian flowered parasol; 7½in (19cm).

WON 782   **WON 700**

WON 790 Bridal pair under plumed vault; 7½in (19cm).

WON 791 Pink garlanded couple; 6½in (16.5cm).

WON 103 Dancing couple encircled by tulle and flowers; 6 x 5in (15 x 12cm).

WON 120 Pink arch with bride and groom set on white steps; 7in (17.8cm).

WON 790   **WON 791**

WON 121 Modern filigree sculpted couple surrounded by arch of flowers; 8½in (21.6cm).

WON 786 Simple traditional bride and groom; 5¾in (14.7cm). Also WON 795.

WON 101 Dancing couple bedecked with peach roses; 4½ x 4½in (11.4 x 11.4cm).

WON 100 Bride and groom on traditional red carpet under white boughs; 7in (17.8cm). Also WON 798.

WON 121   **WON 786**

WON 793

WON 103   WON 120

WON 101   WON 100

WON 106	Gold vase with cream bouquet; 8½in (21.6cm).
WON 32PI	Pink bouquet in slender silver vase; 8½in (21.6cm).
WON 794	Silver vessel festooned in a profusion of pink flowers; 9½in (24.1cm).
WON 32WH	White bouquet in slender silver vase; 8½in (21.6cm). Also WON 118.

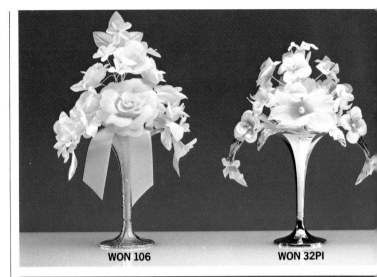

WON 106   **WON 32PI**

WON 108	A loving symbol of red roses in a silver chalice; 9½in (24.1cm).
WON 109	Delicate forget-me-nots set amid an elegant floral arrangement; 9½in (24.1cm).
WON 114	Dainty vase of pink flowers; 6½in (16.5cm).
WON 785	Graceful silvered vase, based on a Victorian pattern, filled with white flowers and leaves; 8½in (21.6cm). Also WON 796.
WON 107	Gold vase, and bouquet for a golden moment; 10½in (26.7cm).

WON 108   **WON 109**

GOLD AND SILVER LACE BANDING

BND 68	Gold 2in (5cm).
BND 69	Silver 2in (5cm).
BND 66	Gold 1½in (3.8cm).
BND 67	Silver 1½in (3.8cm).
BND 64	Gold 1in (2.5cm).
BND 65	Silver 1in (2.5cm).
BND 62	Gold ½in (1.2cm).
BND 63	Silver ½in (1.2cm).

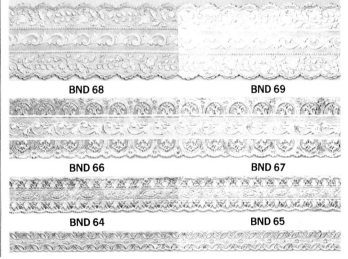

BND 68   **BND 69**

BND 66   **BND 67**

BND 64   **BND 65**

BND 62   **BND 63**

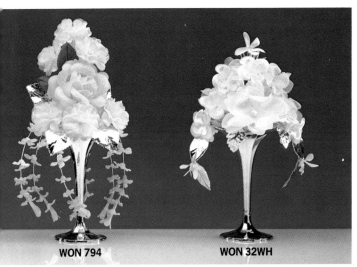

WON 794   WON 32WH

WON 114   WON 785   WON 107

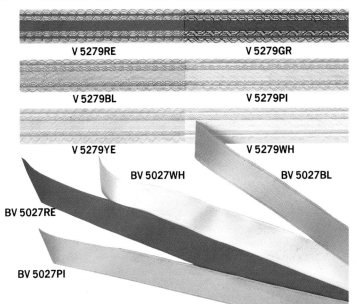

V 5279RE   V 5279GR

V 5279BL   V 5279PI

V 5279YE   V 5279WH

BV 5027WH   BV 5027BL

BV 5027RE

BV 5027PI

DECORETTE RIBBON

V 5279RE	Red.
V 5279GR	Green.
V 5279BL	Blue.
V 5279PI	Pink.
V 5279YE	Yellow.
V 5279WH	White.

SATIN RIBBON

BV 5027BL	Blue with sealed edges; 1in (2.5cm).
BV 5027WH	White with sealed edges; 1in (2.5cm).
BV 5027RE	Red with sealed edges; 1in (2.5cm).
BV 5027PI	Pink with sealed edges; 1in (2.5cm).

71

SUGAR PASTE DECORATIONS

Sugar paste was the basis of Georgian and Victorian cake decorations. Today the delicate sugar tracing is still used in Britain, Germany and Switzerland. The items listed here are very fragile and must be handled with great care. They are backed with fine net and if cracked can still be used.

WON 122 Traditional Victorian vase with up-to-date white bouquet; 9 x 6in (22.8 x 15cm).

WON 122

CU 3	Large ring; $2\frac{1}{2}$ x 2in (6.3 x 5cm).
CU 1	Medium ring; $2\frac{1}{4}$ x $1\frac{1}{2}$in (5.7 x 3.8cm).
CU 4	Small ring; 2 x $1\frac{1}{4}$in (5 x 3.2cm).
C 404	White leaf.
C 502	Blue leaf.
C 41	Leaf.
C 19	Leaf.
C 434	Leaf.
C 433	White leaf; $3\frac{1}{4}$in (8.2cm).
C 500	Blue leaf.
C 101	Leaf.
C 40	Leaf.
C 17	Leaf.
C 51	White cone.
C 501	Blue cone.
C 137	Leaf.
C 18	Leaf.
E 232	White balcony.
C 503	Blue balcony.

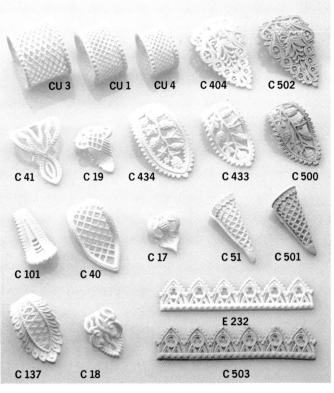

CU 3 CU 1 CU 4 C 404 C 502

C 41 C 19 C 434 C 433 C 500

C 101 C 40 C 17 C 51 C 501

C 137 C 18 E 232 C 503

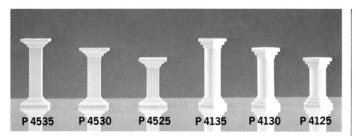

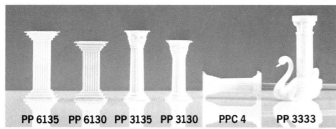

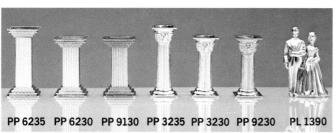

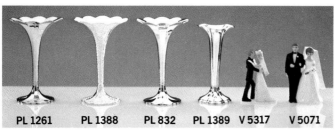

PLASTER PILLARS
The pure white matt finish of these pillars nicely complements the icing of a wedding cake.

P 4535	Square; 3½in (8.9cm).
P 4530	Square; 3in (7.6cm).
P 4525	Square; 2½in (6.3cm).
P 4135	Hexagonal; 3½in (8.9cm).
P 4130	Hexagonal; 3in (7.6cm).
P 4125	Hexagonal; 2½in (6.3cm).

WHITE PLASTIC PILLARS
The material of these pillars is blended to give a white semi-matt finish.

PP 6135	Square; 3½in (8.9cm).
PP 6130	Square; 3in (7.6cm).
PP 3135	Round; 3½in (8.9cm).
PP 3130	Round; 3in (7.6cm).
PPC 4	Pillar and spacer. Ensures stable cake with soft icings.
PP 3333	Swan pillar; 4in (10cm).

METALLISED PILLARS
The metallising process used here gives a finish that does not tarnish.

PP 6235	Square silver; 3½ in (8.9cm).
PP 6230	Square silver; 3in (7.6cm).
PP 9130	Square gold; 3in (7.6cm).
PP 3235	Round silver; 3½in (8.9cm).
PP 3230	Round silver; 3in (7.6cm).
PP 9230	Round gold; 3in (7.6cm).
PL 1390	Silver bride and groom.

VASES
These can be used for floral designs, employing fresh or artificial flowers.

PL 1261	Gold vase; 4⅔in (12cm).
PL 1388	Silver vase with crinkle finish.
PL 832	Silver vase with plain finish.
PL 1389	Silver vase.
V 5317	Dancing bride and groom.
V 5071	Veiled bride with groom.

ROUND CAKE STAND
WV 5185	Round stand. This will take a 14in (35.5cm) round drum or card.

SQUARE CAKE STAND
WV 5186	Square stand. This will take a 14in (35.5cm) square drum or card.

ASSORTED DECORATIONS

CP 2040	Large silver plastic leaf.
CP 2041	Medium silver plastic leaf.
CP 2042	Small silver plastic leaf.
WVS 4540	Silver horseshoe; $1\frac{1}{4}$in (3.2cm).
WVG 4540	Gold horseshoe.
CP 1074	Single heart.
PL 1401	Double heart.
WV 4541	Silver horseshoe; $1\frac{7}{8}$in (4.7cm).
WVS 4527	Silver horseshoe; 1in (2.5cm).
WVG 4527	Gold horseshoe.
CP 1051	Silver bow.
PL 1402	Lovers' knot.
CP 1072	Silver horseshoe; $\frac{1}{2}$in (1.2cm).
CP 1089	Silver horseshoe; $\frac{3}{4}$in (1.9cm).
CP 1090	Gold horseshoe.
CP 1034	Wishbone.
CP 1032	Double bell.
CP 1033	Bell in horseshoe.
CP 1023	Dove on silver horseshoe.
CP 1024	Dove on gold horseshoe.
V 5229	Paper cupids.
CP 1088	Small silver dove.
CP 1026	Dove on silver ring.
CP 1027	Dove on gold ring.
CP 1052	Silver plastic cupids – left and right facing.
CP 1010	Large matt white dove.
CP 1011	Medium matt white dove.
CP 1012	Small matt white dove.

Add your own touch of originality by filling slippers and cones with small flowers or sprays.

WV 4609	Silver slipper.
V 5187	Wishing well.
PL 748	Medium silver bell.
PL 781	Small silver bell.
CP 1050	Silver cone; 2in (5cm).
PL 1338	Church.
PL 1400	Large bell.

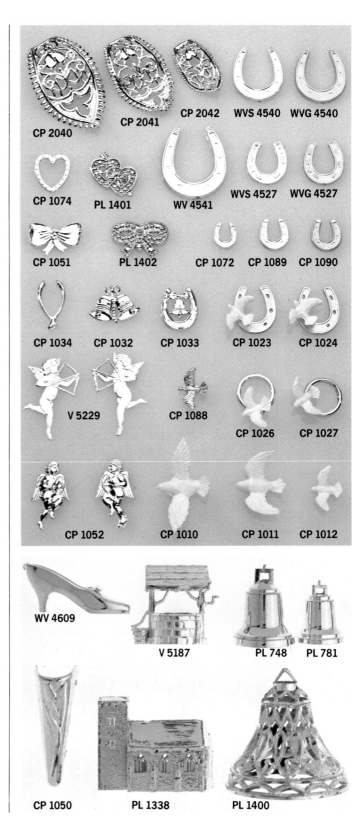

CP 2040 CP 2041 CP 2042 WVS 4540 WVG 4540

CP 1074 PL 1401 WV 4541 WVS 4527 WVG 4527

CP 1051 PL 1402 CP 1072 CP 1089 CP 1090

CP 1034 CP 1032 CP 1033 CP 1023 CP 1024

V 5229 CP 1088 CP 1026 CP 1027

CP 1052 CP 1010 CP 1011 CP 1012

WV 4609 V 5187 PL 748 PL 781

CP 1050 PL 1338 PL 1400

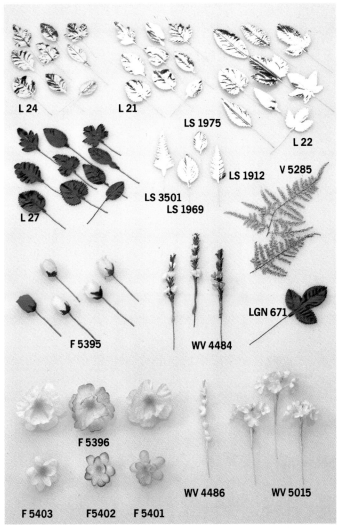

L 24

L 21

LS 1975

L 22

V 5285

LS 1912

LS 3501

LS 1969

L 27

LGN 671

F 5395

WV 4484

F 5396

WV 4486

WV 5015

F 5403   F5402   F 5401

L 1912

L 1886

L 1903

L 303

WV 4701

L 302

L 301

WV 4702

L 312

LEAVES AND FERNS

Here are a few of the many components that you can use to make up your own unique decorations.

L 24	Small gold, assorted.
L 21	Small silver, assorted.
L 22	Large silver, assorted.
L 27	Small green, assorted.
LS 3501	Medium silver fern; 4in (10cm).
LS 1969	Large single silver rose.
LS 1975	Small single rose.
LS 1912	Small silver fern.
V 5285	Asparagus fern.
LGN 671	Green rose leaf.

ROSEBUDS

A place card looks so much prettier embellished with a flower or rosebud.

F 5395RE	Red; $3\frac{1}{2}$in (8.9cm).
F 5395PI	Pink.
F 5395WH	White.
F 5395BL	Blue.
F 5395YE	Yellow.

HEATHER

A sprig of heather makes an excellent good-luck souvenir for wedding guests.

WV 4484WH	White; 5in (12.7cm).
WV 4484PI	Pink.
WV 4484BL	Blue.
WV 4484AS	Assorted.

CLOTH FLOWERS

F 5396WH	Large white; 2in (5cm).
F 5396BL	Large blue.
F 5396PI	Large pink.
F 5403	Small white blossom; $1\frac{1}{2}$in (3.8cm).
F5402	Small blue blossom.
F 5401	Small pink blossom.
WV 4486	Lily of the valley; $5\frac{1}{2}$in (13.9cm).
WV 5015BL	Blue forget-me-nots.
WV 5015PI	Pink forget-me-nots.
WV 5015WH	White forget-me-nots.

UNWIRED LEAVES

L 1912	Small silver fern.
L 1886	Large silver fern.
L 1903	Filigree silver; $1\frac{1}{2}$in (3.8cm).
L 303	Large silver rose.
L 302	Medium silver rose.
WV 4701	Mini gold rose.
L 301	Small silver rose.
WV 4702	Mini silver rose.
L 312	Large gold rose.

FLOWER SPRAYS

Matching sets are available for two and three-tier cakes.

S 52	2 silver leaves with a bell-shaped white flower; 2¾in (7cm).
S 54	2 silver leaves with 3 white flowers and a bow.
S 55	3 silver leaves with 2 white flowers and a bow.
S 6025	Apricot spray with heather, roses and gold leaves.
S 6124	Ring of white and pink flowers.
S 6118	Ring of flowers with green leaves.
S 6107	2 small white flowers with 2 silver fern leaves.
S 6106	Small white flower with 2 silver fern leaves.
S 6105	Small white flower with a silver fern leaf.
S 6131	Slipper, small white blossom and fern leaf.
S 5857	Single white rose with 1 silver leaf.
S 5858	Single white rose with 2 silver leaves.
S 5859	Single white rose with 3 silver leaves.
S 3089	3 small blossoms with 3 silver leaves and a bow.
S 3088	2 small blossoms with 2 silver leaves and a bow.
S 3087	1 small blossom with 1 silver leaf and a bow.
S 198	Slipper with 2 small blossoms and 1 leaf.
S 3082	Horseshoe with small blossoms and 1 silver leaf.

POLYESTER BLOSSOM

Polyester flowers, often known as 'silk' flowers, are almost uncrushable.

S 6112PI	Large pink with 1 leaf; 2in (5cm).
S 6113PI	Large pink with 2 leaves.
S 6114PI	Large pink with 3 leaves.
S 6122	Small pink with 3 silver rose leaves; 1¾in (4.4cm).
S 6121	Small white with 3 silver rose leaves.
S 6123	Small blue with 3 silver rose leaves.

S 52   S 54   S 55

S 6107   S 6106   S 6105   S 6131

S 3089   S 3088   S 3087   S 198

S 274

S 272WH   S 270WH   S 269WH

S 272PI   S 6109YE   S 6109RE

S 6110WH   S 6109WH   S 6108WH

S 6025 · S 6124 · S 6118 · S 5857 · S 5858 · S 5859 · S 3082 · S 6112PI · S 6113PI · S 6114PI · S 273 · S 6122 · S 6121 · S 6123 · S 6108BL · S 6109BL · S 6110BL · S 6108PI · S 6109PI · S 6110PI

HEATHERS

S 272WH	White double with 2 silver leaves and a bow; 4in (10cm).
S 270WH	White double with 2 silver leaves.
S 269WH	White single with 2 silver leaves.
S 274	Slipper with heather and 1 leaf.
S 273	Horseshoe with heather and 1 leaf.
S 272PI	Pink double heather with 2 silver leaves and a bow.

ROSES

S 6109YE	Yellow double with leaves and bow; $3\frac{1}{2}$in (8.9cm).
S 6109RE	Red double, leaves and bow.
S 6108BL	Blue single, leaf and bow.
S 6109BL	Blue double, leaves and bow.
S 6110BL	Blue treble, leaves and bow.
S 6110WH	White treble, leaves and bow.
S 6109WH	White double, leaves and bow.
S 6108WH	White single, leaf and bow.
S 6108PI	Pink single, leaf and bow.
S 6109PI	Pink double, leaves and bow.
S 6110PI	Pink treble, leaves and bow.

ANNIVERSARY ORNAMENTS
All supplied in display packaging.

SN 108	25th Anniversary white floral; 4¼in (10.8cm).
SN 109	30th Anniversary pink floral.
SN 107	Happy Anniversary lilac floral
SN 114	'25' Engraved silver horseshoe.
SN 115	Happy Anniversary silver horseshoe.

SN 108   SN 109   SN 107

SN 110	40th Anniversary red floral.
SN 111	50th Anniversary gold floral.
SN 106	Congratulations pink floral.
SN 113	'40' silver horseshoe and base.
SN 112	'50' golden horseshoe and base.

SN 110   SN 111   SN 106

SPRAYS
Add your own motto to suit the occasion.

S 6127	White flower, roses and white leaves; 5in (12.7cm).
S 6129	Lilac flower, roses and white leaves.
S 6125	Red orchid and rose spray.
S 6126	Pink flower, roses and white leaves.
S 6128	Cream flower, roses and white leaves.
S 6130WH	Large white flower and bow.
S 6130PI	Large pink flower and bow.

S 6127   S 6129

S 6126   S 6128

SN 114   SN 115

SN 113   SN 112

S 6125

S 6130WH   S 6130PI   '21' motto

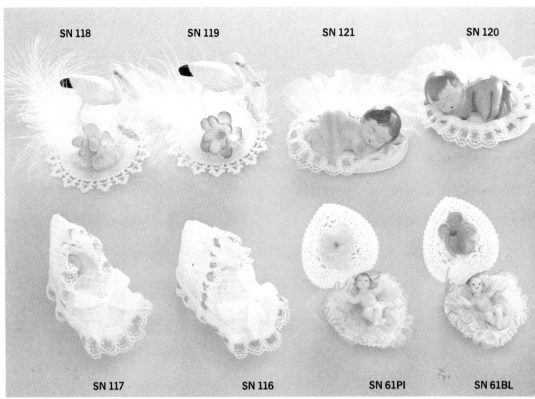

SN 118 SN 119 SN 121 SN 120

SN 117 SN 116 SN 61PI SN 61BL

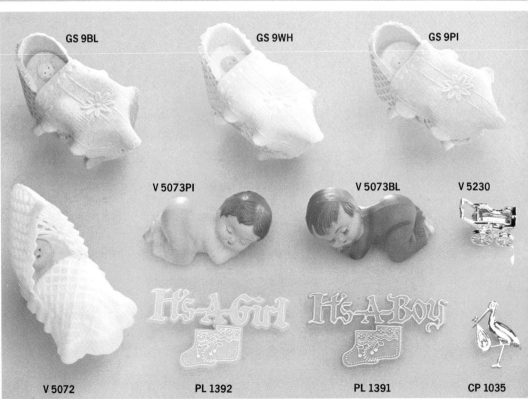

GS 9BL GS 9WH GS 9PI

V 5073PI V 5073BL V 5230

V 5072 PL 1392 PL 1391 CP 1035

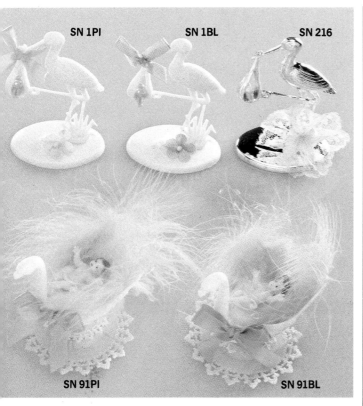

SN 1PI   SN 1BL   SN 216

SN 91PI   SN 91BL

CHRISTENING ORNAMENTS
All supplied in display packaging.

SN 118	Stork with delicate feather and pink flower; 4 x 3in (10 x 7.6cm).
SN 119	Stork with delicate feather and blue flower.
SN 121	Sleeping baby pillowed in fine blue net; 4 x 2in (10 x 5cm).
SN 120	Sleeping baby pillowed in fine pink net.
SN 1PI	Stork with pink flower and bow.
SN 1BL	Stork with blue flower and bow.
SN 1ASS	Stork with flower and bow in assorted colours (not shown).
SN 216	Silver stork.
SN 117	Basket cradle with pink ribbon.
SN 116	Basket cradle with blue ribbon.
SN 61PI	Filigree heart with baby and pink flower.
SN 61BL	Filigree heart with baby and blue flower.
SN 91PI	Baby on swan's back, pink.
SN 91BL	Baby on swan's back, blue.

GS 9BL	Blue sugar paste cradle; 2½in (6.3cm).
GS 9WH	White sugar paste cradle.
GS 9PI	Pink sugar paste cradle.
GS 24PI	Pink sugar paste stork; 3¾in (9.5cm).
GS 24WH	White sugar paste stork.
GS 24BL	Blue sugar paste stork.
V 5072	White plastic cradle.
V 5073PI	Pink sleeping baby.
V 5073BL	Blue sleeping baby.
V 5230	Small silver pram.
PL 1392	It's-A-Girl motto.
PL 1391	It's-A-Boy motto.
CP 1035	Small silver stork.
GP 116	White plastic cradle with bow. Assorted colours.

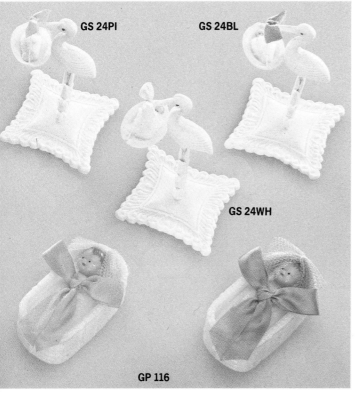

GS 24PI   GS 24BL

GS 24WH

GP 116

18TH AND 21ST BIRTHDAY ORNAMENTS

SN 104	18th pink floral ornament; 4¼in (10.8cm).
SN 124	Metal cast vintage car with Congratulations message on oval base.
SN 105	21st pink floral ornament.
SN 122	White and silver horseshoe with 18th key and pink spray.
SN 123	White and silver horseshoe with 21st key and pink spray.

BIRTHDAY SPRAYS, MOTTOES AND NUMERALS

S 6103BL	Blue 18th birthday spray; 6in (15cm).
S 6103PI	Pink 18th birthday spray.
PL 1252	18th filigree key in silver plastic.
PL 1253	21st filigree key in silver plastic.
S 6102BL	Blue 21st birthday spray.
S 6102PI	Pink 21st birthday spray.
CP 1084	Gold plastic Congratulations.
CP 1056	Silver plastic Congratulations.
CP 1070	Plastic Engagement motto.
CP 1066	Plastic Best Wishes motto.
PL 1209	Blue plastic Happy Birthday.
PL 1208	Pink plastic Happy Birthday.
CP 1053	Silver plastic Happy Birthday.
CP 1054	Plastic Happy Anniversary motto.
CP 1082	Gold plastic Happy Birthday.
PL 1315	White and silver plastic Happy Birthday.
PL 1346	18th plaque; 2½in (6.3cm).
PL 1347	21st plaque.
PL 1348	25th plaque.
PL 1349	30th plaque.
PL 1350	40th plaque.
PL 1351	50th plaque.
CP 1060	Small 18th silver plastic key; 3in (7.6cm).
CP 1059	Small 21st silver plastic key.

SN 104   SN 124   SN 105

S 6103BL   S 6103PI   PL 1252

CP 1084   CP 1056   CP 1066

CP 1070   CP 1060

CP 1059

PL 1346   PL 1347   PL 1348   CP 1085

PL 1349   PL 1350   PL 1351   BV 5318

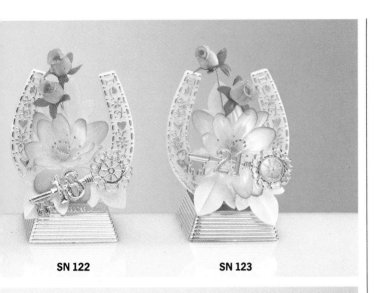

SN 122　　　　　SN 123

PL 1253　　　S 6102BL　　　S 6102PI

PL 1209　　　CP 1053　　　CP 1082

PL 1208　　　CP 1054　　　PL 1315

PL 1292-1301

PL 1399　　PL 1393　PL 1394　PL 1395　PL 1396　PL 1397　PL 1398

CP 1085	Small 21st gold plastic key.
BV 5318	Silver paper Happy Birthday.
	Silver and white numerals; 1in (2.5cm).
PL 1292	No 0.
PL 1293	No 1.
PL 1294	No 2.
PL 1295	No 3.
PL 1296	No 4.
PL 1297	No 5.
PL 1298	No 6.
PL 1299	No 7.
PL 1300	No 8.
PL 1301	No 9.
PL 1399	Silver letters and numerals set.
PL 1393	18th silver numerals.
PL 1394	21st silver numerals.
PL 1395	25th silver numerals.
PL 1396	30th silver numerals.
PL 1397	40th silver numerals.
PL 1398	50th silver numerals.

CANDLES AND PARTY DECORATIONS

PL 1408	Clip-in candle holder (not shown).
ST 2344AS	Assorted candy striped candles.
ST 2404	Numeral candles (not shown).
ST 2403	Magic candles (not shown).
PL 885	Engine candle holders in assorted colours.
PL 886	Carriage candle holders in assorted colours.
PL 1406	Assorted sporting animal candle holders in red and blue.
	Candle holders.
CH 2AS	Assorted
CH 2BL	Blue
CH 2PI	Pink
CH 2RE	Red
CH 2WH	White
CH 2YE	Yellow
V 5213	Large motor bike; 4in (10cm).
PL 1313	Small silver motor bike; 2¼in (5.7cm).
BV 5149	Delicate butterflies, available in a pink, blue and white assortment.
BV 5324	Attractive and novel wooden doll.
BV 5321	Small plastic bear.
PX 508	Plaster bear.
BV 4787	Horse and rider.
BV 5319	Assorted circus animals.
PL 1403	Assorted sporting animal figures in red and blue. Also available as candle holders (PL 1406, above).

HAPPY BIRTHDAY FRILLS

FR 1004BL	Blue frill with printed gold Happy Birthday; 3¼in (8.2cm).
FR 1004PI	Pink frill with printed gold Happy Birthday.
FR 1004WH	White frill with printed gold Happy Birthday.
FR 644BL	Blue floral frill printed Happy Birthday.
FR 644PI	Pink floral frill printed Happy Birthday.
FR 627PL	Blue frill with silver centre band.
FR 627PI	Pink frill with silver centre band.
FR 627WH	White frill with silver centre band.

PL 886
PL 885
BV 5149
BV 478...
V 5213
BV 5324
BV 5321
PX 5...
PL 1313
PL 1357
BV 5320
V 5218
V5219
BFL 14
V 5220
BFC 22

FR 1004BL   FR 1004PI   FR 1004WH

FR 644BL   FR 644PI

FR 627PL   FR 627PI   FR 627WH

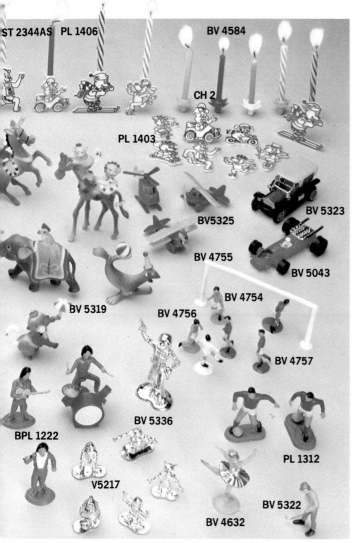

ST 2344AS   PL 1406

BV 4584

CH 2

PL 1403

BV5325

BV 5323

BV 4755

BV 5043

BV 4754

BV 5319

BV 4756

BV 4757

BPL 1222

BV 5336

PL 1312

V5217

BV 5322

BV 4632

	Candles.	
BV 4584AS	Assorted	
BV 4584BL	Blue	
BV 4584PI	Pink	
BV 4584RE	Red	
BV 4584WH	White	
BV 4584YE	Yellow	
BV5325	Assorted aircraft.	
BV 5323	Vintage car; 2½in (6.3cm).	
BV 5043	Racing car.	
PL 1357	Assorted cricketers.	
V 5218	Horse.	
V 5220	Cowboys.	
V5219	Indians.	
BFL 14	Life Guards.	
BV 5320	Assorted musical gnomes.	
BFC 22	Bo-Peep with 2 sheep.	
BPL 1222	Pop group set.	
BV 5336	Large silver spacemen.	
V5217	Small assorted space figures.	
BV 4755	Goalpost.	
	Small footballers.	
BV 4756AS	Assorted	
BV 4756BL	Blue	
BV 4756RE	Red	
BV 4757	Team of players with goalkeeper and posts.	
BV 4754	Goalkeeper.	
PL 1312	Large footballers.	
BV 4632	Ballet dancer.	
BV 5322	Golfer.	
PX 1165	Assorted plaster animals.	

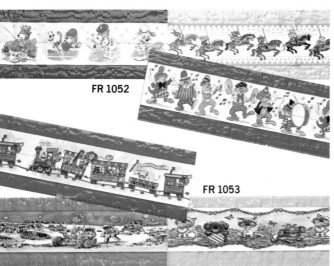

FR 1052

FR 1053

ASSORTED FRILLS

FR 1052	Sporting animals, clowns, horses.
FR 1053	Space figures, trains, cats, dogs.

CRINOLINE LADIES

Create a special Crinoline Lady cake with these plaster figurines. The one with the spike is designed for use with soft sponge cakes.

PX 1150	Crinoline Lady with hat; 3½in (8.9cm).
PX 1162	Crinoline Lady with spike.

WALT DISNEY DECORATIONS

Add atmosphere to a party with the children's favourite Walt Disney characters. For details of candles, see pages 86–87.

PL 1233	Assorted red and blue Disney candle holders; $4\frac{3}{4} \times 3\frac{1}{4}$in (12 x 8.2cm).
WFL 121	Snow White and Seven Dwarfs waferettes.
CF 51	Assorted Disney sugar pipings.

ASSORTED DISNEY WAFERETTES

WFL 20	Assorted.
WFL 16	Donald Duck.
WFL 17	Mickey Mouse.
WFL 18	Pluto.
WFL 19	Daisy Duck.
WFL 15	Minnie Mouse.
WFL 217	Goofy.
EMB 940	Mickey and Minnie Happy Birthday wafer plaque; 4in (10cm).
FR 925	Disney frills. ; $3\frac{1}{4}$in (8.2cm).

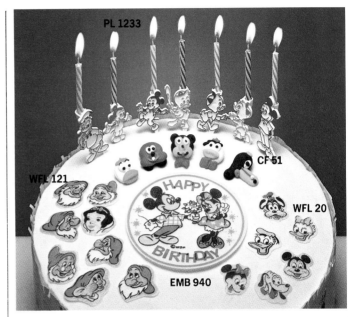

These new designs make wonderful decorations or toys – as well as a popular party souvenir.

BV 5327	Donald Duck; 2in (5cm).
BV 5328	Goofy.
BV 5330	Mickey Mouse and ball.
BV 5329	Minnie Mouse.
BV 5326	Mickey Mouse.

EASTER EGGS

Traditionally these eggs are filled with sweets, toys or petits fours.

V 5282	Red and gold foil eggs with clear lids; 5in (12.7cm).
V 5281	Red and gold foil eggs.
V 4900	Cardboard picture egg; 5in (12.7cm).
V 4901	Cardboard picture egg; 6in (15cm).

V 5282

V 5281

V 4900

V 4901

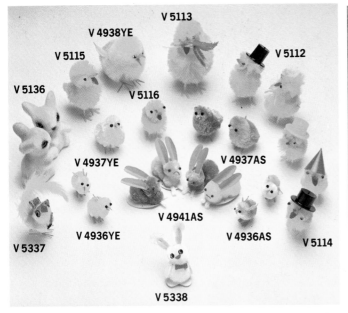

DECORATIONS FOR EASTER AND MOTHER'S DAY

V 5112	Chicks – bride and groom; 2½in (6.3cm).
V 5113	Large chenille chick.
V 4938YE	Large yellow chenille chick.
V 5115	Medium chenille chick.
V 5114	Medium chenille chick with hat.
V 4937AS	Medium chicks in assorted colours.
V 5116	Small chenille chick.
V 4937YE	Medium yellow chenille chick.
V 5136	Assorted flock bunnies.
V 4936AS	Small chicks in assorted colours; 1in (2.5cm).
V 4941AS	Assorted chenille rabbits.
V 4936YE	Small yellow chenille chicks.
V 5337	Yellow chenille chick with feather and hat.
V 5338	White chenille rabbit.

FR 1030YE	Happy Easter frill.

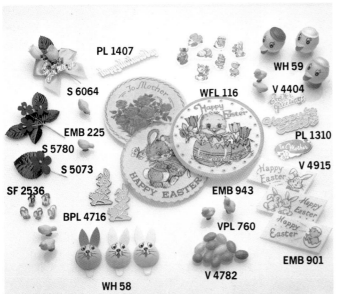

PL 1407	Gold plastic Mother's Day motto; 3⅝in (9.2cm).
WFL 116	Easter waferettes.
WH 59	Assorted Easter chick wafer heads.
S 5780	Large violet spray.
S 5073	Single violet spray.
S 6064	Yellow rose spray with Easter greetings motto.
EMB 225	Mother's Day plaque.
EMB 943	Happy Easter plaque.
VPL 760	Assorted plastic Easter chicks in 3 positions.
V 4404	Green and gold foil Happy Easter motto.
PL 1310	Yellow and gold Happy Easter motto.
V 4915	To Mother motto.
SF 2536	Mini sweet peas in sugar.
BPL 4716	Pink and blue rabbits.
WH 58	Wafer rabbit heads.
V 4782	Fondant eggs.
EMB 901	Easter wafer mottoes.

CULOTS AND WAFERETTES

Culots add realism to marzipan fruits and other sweets and candies.

QL 13	Apple culot; ¾in (1.9cm).
PL 800	Large strawberry culot.
PL 900	Small strawberry culot.
WFL 75	Halloween waferettes.

WAFERS

Wafer or 'rice paper' is edible and blends into icing and anything that is not too wet.

EMB 939	Beautiful wafer plaque 4in (10cm).

The two next wafer items have many uses on cakes small and large, on ice creams, jellies and biscuits.

WFL 115	Circus waferettes.
WH 56	5 amusing wafer heads.

EMB 939

WFL 115

WH 56

SUGAR FLOWERS

SF 161	Assortment of sugar flowers; $1\frac{1}{4}$in (3.2cm).
SF 7	Multi-coloured 6 petal flowers with coloured centres; 1in (2.5cm).
	Roses; $1\frac{1}{4}$in (3.2cm).
SF 22AS	Assorted
SF 22PE	Peach
SF 22PI	Pink
SF 22RE	Red
SF 22WH	White
SF 22YE	Yellow
	Roses; 1in (2.5cm).
SF 19AS	Assorted
SF 19RE	Red
SF 19WH	White
SF 3000	Pansies.
SF 96	Small twist sugar flowers; $\frac{1}{2}$in (1.2cm).
	Roses; $\frac{3}{4}$ (1.9cm).
SF 26AS	Assorted
SF 26PE	Peach
SF 26PI	Pink
SF 26RE	Red
SF 26WH	White
SF 26YE	Yellow
SF 121	Large violets.
SF 2537	Small violets.
SUG 907	A Happy Birthday sugar plaque.

SF 161

SF 7

SF 96

SF 3000

SF 121

SF 2537

SUG 907

SF 120

SUG 933

CF 9

WE 22

WE 20

L 326   **L325**

WE 21

WAFER ROSES

Wafer roses, with their delicate petals and attractive colours, make a delightful alternative to the sugar rose.

	Large ; 2in (5cm).
WE 22AS	Assorted
WE 22BL	Blue
WE 22PI	Pink
WE 22RE	Red
WE 22WH	White
WE 22YE	Yellow
	Medium ; 1½in (3.8cm).
WE 21AS	Assorted
WE 21BL	Blue
WE 21PI	Pink
WE 21RE	Red
WE 21WH	White
WE 21YE	Yellow
	Small ; 1in (2.5cm).
WE 20AS	Assorted
WE 20BL	Blue
WE 20OR	Orange
WE 20PI	Pink
WE 20RE	Red
WE 20TE	Tea
WE 20WH	White
WE 20YE	Yellow
L 326	Large green wafer leaf.
L325	Small green wafer leaf.

SF 120	Narcissus.
SF 2532	Mini sugar roses.
SF 101	Assorted sugar flowers.
CF 12	Rabbit pipings.
SUG 933	Sugarettes.
CF 9	Assorted sugar pipings – ideal for small children's cakes and desserts.
SF 420	Very small sugar stars.
SB 121	Sugar figure plaques – delightful hand-painted items used on a 'royal cake'.

SF 22

SF 19

SF 26

SF 2532

SF 420   **SF 101**   **CF 12**   **SB 121**

CHRISTMAS FIGURES

These can be used to decorate not only cakes, but your house and Christmas tree also.

V 5226	Mr and Mrs Santa kissing; 2½in (6.3cm).
PL 765	Snow covered house and tree.
CV 5331	Small Christmas animal figures.
CV 5332	Assorted happy children.
PL 842	Father Christmas with sack of parcels.
PL 763	Signpost to Merry Xmas.
PL 837	Father Christmas on skis.
PL 733	Father Christmas waving.
PL 737	Reindeer – on its own or with the next item.
PL 784	Father Christmas on sledge.
PL 2	Father Christmas – a simple and inexpensive version of Santa.
PL 1017	Father Christmas with painted face and extra detail.
PL 1282	Snowboys on toboggans, throwing snowballs and skiing.
CV 4932	Snowman and toys.
PL 767	Snowman with hat, broom and scarf.

TREES AND PLASTER FIGURES

TNP 20	Green fibre tree, no pot; 2in (5cm).
TWP 15	Green fibre tree with pot; 1½in (3.8cm).
TNP 15	Green fibre tree, no pot; 1½in (3.8cm).
TWP 20	Green fibre tree with pot; 2in (5cm).
PX 29	Plaster chalet.
PX 25	Medium plaster Father Christmas.
PX 1164	Plaster Christmas mouse.
PX 1161	Father Christmas in chimney pot.
EMB 942	Oblong wafer mottoes in assorted designs.
PX 1163	Plaster Father Christmas with Christmas tree.
PX 700	Modern comic Father Christmas.
PX 26	Plaster Father Christmas with sack.
PX 32	Small plaster Father Christmas.
PX 215	Jolly plaster snowman.
PX 27	Small snowman.
EMB 941	Happy Christmas wafer plaque; 4¾in (12cm).
WH 57	Wafer Father Christmas head.

CV 5332

PL 1282

PL 827

V 5225

PL 600

CV 4931

CV 4933	Children and snowmen.
PL 601	Light brown robin for the traditional Yuletide log cake.
PL 827	Robin on a log.
PL 600	Dark brown robin.
V 5225	Father Christmas skating.
CV 4931	Carol singers.

These windows and doors are useful for all kinds of houses, chalets and novelty ideas such as the helicopter cake shown earlier in the section on Birthday Cakes.

LA 79	Wafer windows.
LA 80	Wafer doors.
LA 72	Wafer log ends.

CF 27	Assorted sugar pipings.
SUG 947	Oval sugar plaques in 3 designs; 2¾in (7cm).
PL 1026	Axe for the Christmas log.
PL 1260	Assorted metallised bells in red, green, gold, blue.
CV 5333	Green plastic Christmas tree.
CV 5334	Silver plastic Christmas tree.
CV 5335	Gold plastic Christmas tree.
PL 875	Green plastic tree with snow.
SUG 946	Oblong sugar Merry Christmas motto.
WFL 119	Assorted Christmas waferettes.
PX 1159	Plaster robin.

PX 1164

PX 25

PX 1161

EMB 942

PX 1163

PX 700

PX 32

PX 26

SUG 947

PL 1026

CV 5333

CV 5335

CV 5334

PL 1260

PL 875

HOLLY SPRAYS

The new plastic range, HP 2027-2036, is particularly realistic in shape and colour. With paper holly care must be taken to ensure that icings are dry before and after application.
(H = Paper. HP = Plastic).

HP 1919	Gold Merry Christmas and large green 5 leaf spray.
HP 2034	Spray, Happy Christmas motto with cluster of holly and berries.
HP 2033	Spray, Happy Christmas motto and 2 leaves.
HP 1853	Complete log cake decoration.
H 1519	Spray, 3 leaves, 2 red berries and robin.
HP 2027	Spray, 3 leaves, red bow and lantern.
H 2217	Spray, triple gold and green leaves and 3 red roses.
H 2249	Spray, 5 pointed gold and red foil leaves and gold berries.
HP 2035	Spray, 3 gold metallised leaves, red bow and gold berries.
HP 2029	Spray, 3 leaves, red bow and gold berries.
HP 2036	Small and medium metallised leaves.
HP 2032	Spray, 3 leaves, 3 berries and white flower.
HP 2030	Spray, 3 leaves, red bow and gold double bell.
HP 2028	Spray, 3 leaves, red bow and red berries.
H 8	Spray, 2 leaves and 2 red berries.
H 9	Spray, 3 leaves and 3 red berries.
H 102	5 pointed piquet.
H 12	Spray, 5 leaves and 5 red berries.
H 3	Small triple piquet.
H 2	Medium triple piquet.
H 1	Large triple piquet.
HP 101	Large quadruple piquet.
HP 1533	Small triple piquet.
HP 1532	Medium triple piquet.
HP 1531	Large triple piquet.
HP 1885	Large 5 pointed piquet.

CHRISTMAS FRILLS

FR 1002	Assorted Christmas frills printed on foil; 3¼in (8.2cm).
FR 1040	Assorted red frills with traditional designs printed on silver centre bands.
FR 1041	Assorted narrow frills for smaller cakes; 2½in (6.3cm).

HP 1919   HP 2034   HP 2033

HP 1853   H 1519   HP 2027

H 2217   H 2249   HP 2035   HP 2029

HP 2036   HP 2032   HP 2030   HP 2028

H 8   H 9   H 102   H 12

H 3   H 2   H 1   HP 101   HP 1885

HP 1533   HP 1532   HP 1531

FR 1002

FR 1040

FR 1041

PL 1404 | PL 976 | PL 909

HL 1315 | PL 1264 | PL 1265

CV 2192 | CV 4383 | CV 4448

CV 4382 | CV 4533 | CC 1 | CC 3

CV 4508 | CV 5193

CV 5192 | PL 973

BND 78 | BND 79 | BND 80

FR 1054

FR 1016 | FR 602 | FR 909

CHRISTMAS DECORATIONS

PL 1404	Red metallised Merry Christmas motto.
PL 976	Red plastic Merry Christmas.
PL 909	Metallised gold plastic Merry Christmas.
HL 1315	Silver foil and card axe.
PL 1264	Happy Christmas blocked in gold on red plastic.
PL 1265	Happy Christmas with robin and lantern.
CV 2192	Foil Merry Christmas in an oval holly wreath.
CV 4383	Foil Merry Christmas on round wreath.
CV 4448	Foil Merry Christmas with robin.
CV 4382	Foil Merry Christmas with holly.
CV 4533	Foil Seasons Greetings in green, red and gold.
CC 1	Assorted crackers in multi-coloured foil; 3½in (8.9cm).
CC 3	Gold crackers; 2¾in (7cm).
CV 4508	Foil Merry Christmas motto.
CV 5193	Foil Merry Christmas motto.
CV 5192	Seasons Greetings motto with axe.
PL 973	Half relief Father Christmas; 2¾in (7cm).
BND 78	Red banding with embossed edge; 24in (60cm) long.
BND 79	Embossed gold band with 1in (2.5cm) wide red lace banding; 24in (60cm) long.
BND 80	Embossed red band with 1in (2.5cm) wide gold lace banding; 24in (60cm) long.
FR 1054	Assortment of happy and humorous Christmas frills; 3¼in (8.2cm) wide. Matching sugar plaques are shown on page 93.
FR 1016	Red printed Merry Christmas frill; 3¼in (8.2cm).
FR 602	Red tartan frill; 2½in (6.3cm).
FR 909	Red frill with gold centre band; 2½in (6.3cm).

METAL ICING TUBES

Fine quality chromed nickel – no ragged edges or seams.

V 5074	Plain Tube No 2, 1.5mm.
V 5075	Plain Tube No 3, 2mm.
V 5076	Plain Tube No 4, 2.5mm.
V 5077	Plain Tube No 5, 3mm.
V 5078	Plain Tube No 6, 3.5mm.
V 5079	Star Tube No 25, 4mm.
V 5080	Star Tube No 27, 5mm.
V 5081	Star Tube No 29, 6mm.
V 5082	Star Tube No 31, 8mm.
V 5083	Rope Tube No 14, 3mm.
V 5084	Rope Tube No 16, 4mm.
V 5085	Rope Tube No 18, 5mm.
V 5086	Rope Tube No 20, 6mm.
V 5087	Rope Tube No 22, 8mm.
V 5088	Petal Tube No 61, 12mm.
V5089	Flower Tube No 102, 8mm.
V 5090	Flower Tube No 104, 13mm.
V 5091	Petal Tube No 59, 8mm.
V 5092	Leaf Tube No 66, 5mm.
V 5093	Leaf Tube No 68, 7mm.
V 5094	Basket Tube No 47, 8mm.
V 5124	Plain Tube No 0, 0.5mm.
V 5125	Plain Tube No 1, 1mm.
V 5126	Rope Tube No 43, 4mm.
V 5127	Rope Tube No 44, 5mm.

THERMO SAVOY TUBES

Strong non-porous bags which can be boiled to clean.

TV 4862	Round Tube Size 7, 7mm.
TV 4863	Round Tube Size 9, 11mm.
TV 4864	Round Tube Size 11, 13mm.
TV 4865	Round Tube Size 13, 14mm.
TV 4868	Star Tube Size 3, 8mm.
TV 4869	Star Tube Size 5, 9mm.
TV 4871	Star Tube Size 7, 10mm.
TV 4873	Star Tube Size 9, 13mm.
TV 4874	Star Tube Size 11, 16mm.
TV 4875	Star Tube 13, 18mm.
TV 4876	Star Tube Size 15, 20mm.

THERMO SAVOY BAGS

TV 4947	Savoy Bag, 12in.
TV 4948	Savoy Bag, 14in.
TV 4949	Savoy Bag, 16in.
TV 4950	Savoy Bag, 18in.
TV 4952	Savoy Bag, 22in.
TV 4953	Savoy Bag, 24in.

CAKE DECORATING BOOKS

CAT 1, 3, 5	*Creative Cake Decorating Made Easy* – three practical and inexpensive books.
BOK 3	*Cake Designs and Ideas* – over 100 colour plates.
BOK 1	*The Culpitt Book of Cake Decoration.*
BOK 2	Display pack for BOK 1.

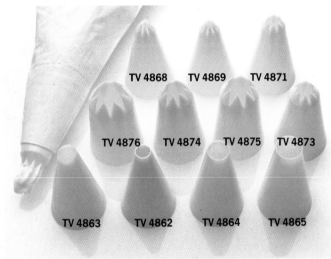

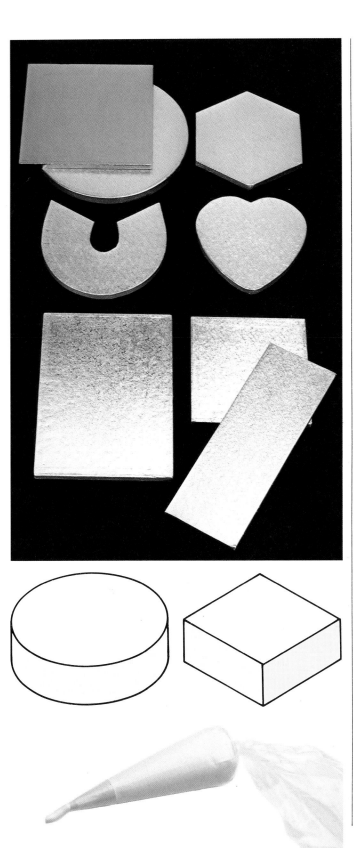

CAKE DRUMS AND CARDS

Cake 'board' is a term often used to describe any base board on which a cake sits. More correctly they should be described as 'drums' or 'cards', depending on their thickness.

Cake Drums Approx. ½in (1.2cm) thick or more. Available in round, square, oblong, hexagonal, horseshoe and heart shapes, and in various thicknesses.

Cake Cards Approx. ¼in (6mm) thick or less. Available in round, square or oblong shapes and in 'single thickness' – approx. ⅛in (3mm) – or 'double thickness' – approx. ¼in (6mm). Also available with turned or cut edges.

HOW TO MEASURE CAKE DRUMS AND CARDS

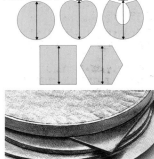

CAKE DUMMIES

These are suitable for Royal or Plastic Icing and make good durable cake bases for exhibition or display pieces. They can be cut with hot wire or a small saw. Available in round or square shapes; 6in (15cm), 8in (20cm) and 10in (25cm).

DISPOSABLE SAVOY BAGS

Disposable Savoy Bags can be used for piping most substances, from fresh cream to sausage meat. Now improved welded seams make them even stronger.

PPW 19 Hygienic Plastic Disposable Savoy Bags.

95

AAAAA BB CC DD EEEEE FF GG HH IIII JJJ KK LL MMM NN N OOO PP RRR SS TT UUU VV WW YY &&&&&&&&&& III2234567889900

DC 11

DE-LUXE QUALITY LETTERS AND NUMERALS
Whatever the event, whatever the occasion, whether it is a Name, Age, Message or Monogram, these new de-luxe quality Letters or Numerals are easy to use and will enhance the product. They are suitable for use on many items from celebration cakes to greetings cards.

DC 11	Letters and Numerals in silver plastic; approx. ³⁄₄in (1.9cm).

ACKNOWLEDGMENTS

G.T. Culpitt & Son Ltd would like to acknowledge, with thanks, the following people, both for their help in designing the cakes in the book and also for their help in reproducing in the UK those cakes designed in other parts of the world.

HOME
Molly Bridle, Wallington, Surrey.
Hazel Brogan, Chaldon, Surrey.
Suzanne Butcher, Cardiff.
D. M. Chandler, Purbrook, Hants.
Barbara Cullen, Felixstowe, Hants.
Janet Hughes, Bromley, Kent.
Jane Jones, Wedding Themes, St. Albans, Herts.
Margaret Morland, Newcastle, Tyne & Wear.
Nightingale Cake Centre, South Woodford, E18.
C. Oatham, Twins Wedding Shop, Chase Cross, Essex.
Diane Parkin, Graveshead, Kent.
Clive Parr, G.T. Culpitt & Son Ltd, Hatfield, Herts.
Margaret Patchin, Twyford, Berks.
J. Anne Pidgeon, Twyford, Berks.

John Sanderson, Head of Bakery and Confectionery section, Monkwearmouth College of Further Education, Sunderland.
Joyce Snell, North Romford, Essex.
Joan Shaw, Twins Wedding Shop, Chase Cross, Essex.
Betty Walker, Stratford-upon-Avon, Warwicks.
Janet Webber, Heathfield, East Sussex.

OVERSEAS
Helen Bennett, Duncraig, W. Australia.
Mary Brunsgard, Balcatta, W. Australia.
Yvonne Przetocki, Hamersley, W. Australia.
Robyn Reed, Stafford, Queensland, Australia.
Carol Young, Arana Hills, Queensland, Australia.
Amy's Cake Shop, Vancouver, Canada.
Henry Han, Win Sin (Pty) Ltd, Singapore.
Karl Hansen, 'Royal' Vestergade 28 DK – 5000 Odense, Denmark.

G.T. Culpitt & Son Ltd would also like to thank the following for their contributions and help in compiling this book:

Joan Burns and **Mavis Atkinson** for designing most of the decorations used and illustrated in the book.
Clive Parr for his patient and practical contributions to all aspects of the production.
Shirley Culpitt for her organization of the international selection of cakes.
The British Sugarcraft Guild.
The following distributors, who were particularly helpful in organizing the international contribution to this book:
Ron and Brenda Petersen, Petersen's Cake Decorations Pty Ltd, Perth, Australia.
Fer and Bernie Lewis, Cake Ornament Co., Brisbane, Australia.
David Cheong, Win Sin (Pty) Ltd, Singapore.
Caryl Chayko, Nicholson Equipment Ltd, Vancouver BC, Canada.
A. Th. Jensen, Odense, Denmark.